To Barbara, Whatley, and
Rose, the inspiration for all
my creative endeavors.

Acknowledgments

Wow, my first four-color book—
I am jazzed. Thanks to Nancy Davis
and Marjorie Baer for inviting me to
join the debut of this new series, and
to Judy Ziajka, who pretty much
whipped this book into shape single-
handedly. Thanks to moto-girl Lisa
Brazieal for all her assistance and
design encouragement (it really
helped), to Myrna Vladic for her end-
of-the-process aid, and to Owen
Wolfson, compositor for this book.

I couldn't write these books without the computers from Dell and
Hewlett-Packard that I exclusively
work on (and recommend highly) or
the software from Microsoft (Word,
PowerPoint, Windows XP, and Movie
Maker), Adobe (InDesign), and Ulead
(PhotoImpact). Special thanks to
Michael Patten and David Caulton
from Microsoft for answering my
frequent, frantic inquiries.

I appreciate the support of those
who came before me, especially
Papa John Buechler, Mr. Movie
Maker himself. Let's hope a rising
tide raises all boats in the harbor.

Once again, thanks to Pat Tracy
for technical and other assistance.

contents

contents

contents

.

introduction

The Visual QuickProject Guide you're reading offers a unique way to learn new skills. Instead of drowning you in long text descriptions, this Visual QuickProject Guide uses color screen shots with clear, concise step-by-step instructions to show you how to complete a project in a matter of hours.

In this book, I'll be creating a movie from the video and digital pictures my wife and I shot of my eldest daughter's last birthday. You'll be working with your own video, which may be a birthday video, but could be video from a vacation, graduation, or any other occasion. However, though the events may be different, the process of editing the video footage and digital pictures into a finished movie will be almost identical. Thus, you can apply the principles you learn here to your own movies—just replace "birthday movie" with the occasion of your choice.

We'll be working with Microsoft's video editor, Microsoft Windows Movie Maker 2. Why Movie Maker? Because it has all the features you need to build an exciting, fun-to-watch movie, and it's free with Windows XP.

what you will learn

You will learn to create a movie using Movie Maker.

You'll start by capturing video from your DV camcorder, which Movie Maker simplifies with its Video Capture wizard.

Movie Maker stores all captured video in the Contents pane.

I'll show you how to drag your clips to the Storyboard and arrange them in the proper order.

Transitions are visual effects that smooth the flow from one scene to another. Movie Maker provides dozens to tickle your creativity; here I'm using the Heart transition. I'll show you how and where to effectively use transitions and special effects.

Time to go (sniff, sniff)

Titles help your viewers understand what's going on in the movie. I'll show you how to choose among Movie Maker's extensive style options and how to change fonts and colors to your liking.

Microphone

Movie Maker makes it easy to add background music and narration (it's her birthday, so she's telling the story).

You'll learn how to add these audio elements and how to make them work smoothly with the audio captured with your camcorder.

introduction

what you will learn (cont.)

My wife is a digital camera fanatic, and I like adding her pictures to the movie, which is a snap in Movie Maker. Here I'm creating a slide show from my wife's digital pictures with my daughter narrating in the background. You'll learn how to create a slide show and set options, such as picture and transition duration, to your liking.

Here's Movie Maker in Timeline view, which, by the way, is a great view for synchronizing titles, audio, and transitions to pictures or video on the top track.

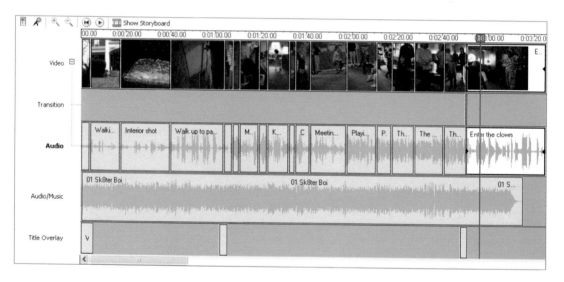

One of Movie Maker's strongest features is AutoMovie, which takes your video and synchronizes it with a song you select to create a music video. You'll learn how and when to create AutoMovies and how they integrate into larger projects.

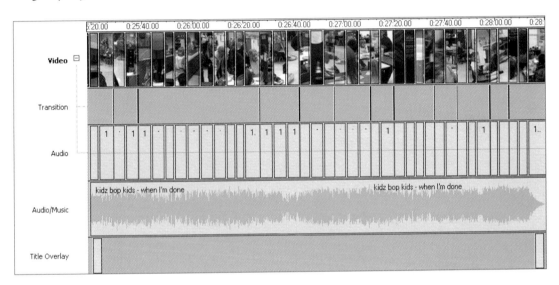

Producing movies is fun, but sending them out to be watched by others is even more fun. You'll learn how to save a video file for viewing on your computer, save your project to a CD, send your movie via e-mail, upload your movie to a Web site, and send your movie back to your DV camera.

You'll also learn how to produce a video file you can use to create a DVD with any number of third-party programs.

how this book works

The title of each section explains what is covered on that page.

fade audio out and in

You just inserted a video transition. Now you'll work on the audio. You'll fade out the audio on the clip before the transition—from 100% volume to 0%—and fade it back in on the clip after the transition—from 0% volume to 100%.

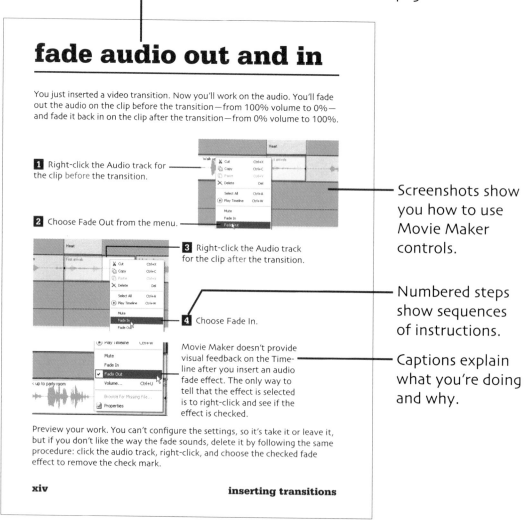

1 Right-click the Audio track for the clip before the transition.

2 Choose Fade Out from the menu.

Screenshots show you how to use Movie Maker controls.

3 Right-click the Audio track for the clip after the transition.

4 Choose Fade In.

Numbered steps show sequences of instructions.

Movie Maker doesn't provide visual feedback on the Timeline after you insert an audio fade effect. The only way to tell that the effect is selected is to right-click and see if the effect is checked.

Captions explain what you're doing and why.

Preview your work. You can't configure the settings, so it's take it or leave it, but if you don't like the way the fade sounds, delete it by following the same procedure: click the audio track, right-click, and choose the checked fade effect to remove the check mark.

xiv

inserting transitions

The extra bits section at the end of each chapter contains tips and tricks that you might like to know, but which aren't absolutely necessary for creating a movie.

extra bits

add background music p. 92

- I use Windows Media Player to copy audio tracks from a CD-ROM so I can include them in a movie. It's very simple to use, but if you want step-by-step guidance, see Microsoft Windows Movie Maker 2: Visual QuickStart Guide from Peachpit Press for details.

- You can also add sound effects to your videos on the Audio/Music track. Although Movie Maker doesn't come with any sound effects or background music, Microsoft offers two free sources of both. The Creativity Fun Pack (http://www.microsoft.com/windowsxp/moviemaker/downloads/create.asp) comes with 53 sound effects in five categories: animal, fun random, graduation, party and sports, and background music. Microsoft's Windows Movie Maker 2 Winter Fun Pack 2003 (http://www.microsoft.com/windowsxp/moviemaker/downloads/winterfun.asp), also free, includes 92 sound effects and 7 music tracks.

set up for narration p. 102

- There's a big difference between the microphone port and the line-in port available on some computers. The line-in port is used for the output from stereo systems and other independently powered devices and requires a significantly stronger signal than you get with the typical computer microphone. Line-in ports won't work with a microphone, so be sure you connect your microphone to the microphone port.

The heading for each group of tips matches the section title.

The page number next to the heading makes it easy to find the section the tips belong to.

tools you will need

Here's what you need to complete the project in this book:

At least 20 GB of free disk space for each hour-long project and a CD-Recordable or CD-Rewritable drive for producing recordable CDs.

A computer running Microsoft Windows XP Professional or Home Edition with a 600-MHz processor, 128 MB of RAM, a sound card, a FireWire card (to capture video from a DV camera), a microphone for narration, and an Internet connection (for sending movies via e-mail or uploading movies to a Web site).

If you produce lots of movies, you'll run out of disk space quickly. If you think you may not have enough space, consider adding another drive to your computer; contact your local computer dealer to find out how.

A digital camcorder with miniDV tapes for shooting video footage and transferring video to and from the computer.

You'll also need some interesting video to work with and some digital photographs and songs.

(Used with permission of Sony Electronics, Inc.)

A FireWire cable to connect the camcorder to the computer.

Blank CD-R discs (if you have a CD recorder and want to burn your movies to CD-R/RW).

(Used with permission of Verbatim Corporation)

Movie Maker 2 downloaded and installed.

You'll use Microsoft Windows Media Player to play your movies once they're produced, but that's installed on every Windows XP computer.

movie maker terms

To make your work in Movie Maker easier, I've defined some of the key terms you'll encounter as you work in the program. We'll be using these terms throughout this book.

- Video: The footage you shoot with your camcorder. It includes both images and audio.

- Movie: The final result that Movie Maker produces when you've finished editing and are ready to share your production.

- Capture: The process of transferring video from your camera to your computer.

- Import: The process of inserting an audio, video, or picture file already on your hard drive into Movie Maker.

- Render: The process Movie Maker goes through in producing a movie.

- Video clip: Video captured or imported into Movie Maker. Video clips include the audio originally shot with the video.

- Audio clip: Separate audio files (usually music) imported into Movie Maker.

- Picture: A still image you shoot with your digital camera and import into Movie Maker.

- Project: The file where Movie Maker stores your work while you're working on a movie. The project file references the video clips, audio clips, and pictures (often collectively referred to as content or assets) you're including in your movie, but Movie Maker doesn't actually copy them into the project file. This keeps the project file small, but it also means that you must be sure not to delete the captured files until after you produce your final movie.

- AutoMovie: A series of video clips that Movie Maker automatically assembles and synchronizes to a background audio clip. You can edit AutoMovies after Movie Maker creates them, and you can add them as components of longer productions or create them as stand-alone movies.

the next step

While this Visual QuickProject Guide will give you an excellent start, there's a lot more to learn about the art of movie making and working with Movie Maker and the excellent suite of additional media creation tools that Microsoft offers. If you're curious, check out my Microsoft Windows Movie Maker 2: Visual QuickStart Guide, also published by Peachpit Press.

The Visual QuickStart Guide features clear examples, concise step-by-step instructions, and lots of helpful tips. It covers every aspect of shooting and capturing video and editing and producing compelling, fun-to-watch movies.

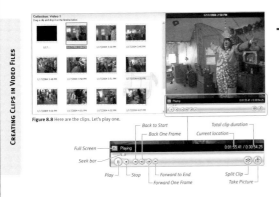

1. welcome to movie maker

Movie Maker is easy to learn, and for the most part, you can use it without having to fiddle with its options or do any elaborate set up. But just as with any new tool you use, it's a good idea to take a quick look around to familiarize yourself with the basic operations. That's what you'll do in this chapter. Then you'll be ready to jump right in and start bringing your video footage into Movie Maker and begin making movies.

So Launch Movie Maker, and let's get underway.

Movie Maker 2 in all its glory.

Producing family videos is fun and rewarding (plus you get to make sure that you're included).

Here's me with Whatley, whose birthday party video will be your model throughout this book.

movie maker tour

You can switch this window between the Collections pane, which houses all your content—your video footage, audio recordings, and still pictures (together known as your project assets)—and the Movie Tasks pane (shown), where you launch Movie Maker functions such as Capture Video and Finish Movie.

The Contents pane contains imported audio, video, and pictures and Movie Maker's libraries of transitions and video effects. Click any item in the Contents pane to preview it in the Monitor.

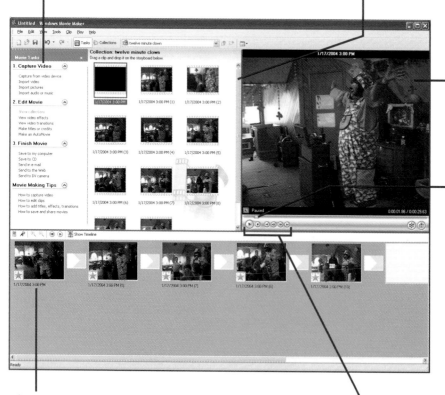

The Monitor displays your content and previews your project.

Use the Seek bar to scroll through your clips.

This is Movie Maker's Storyboard view, which displays each clip in the project in a separate window. Storyboard view is great for arranging your content in the desired order. Once you've arranged your clips, you switch to Timeline view to add titles, transitions, effects, and other audio.

You can control playback with the VCR-like controls at the bottom.

The window now shows the Collections pane with the first imported content (assets) and Movie Maker's Video Effects and Video Transitions collections. Click any collection to view its assets in the Contents pane.

Click the appropriate button to view the Collections pane or Movie Tasks pane. Spend a few moments clicking back and forth between these views to familiarize yourself with them.

The Contents pane showing Movie Maker's Video Transitions collection. Again, click any item to preview it in the Monitor.

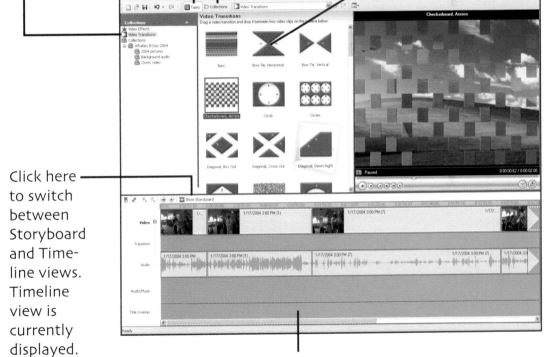

Click here to switch between Storyboard and Timeline views. Timeline view is currently displayed.

This is Movie Maker's Timeline view, a longitudinal view with separate tracks for video, transitions, audio, audio/music (background music or narration), and title overlays (titles).

welcome to movie maker

movie maker tour (cont.)

Now take a quick look at the main toolbar. Once you're familiar with how to view your collections and access Movie Maker's tools, you'll be in great shape to start editing. Don't worry about becoming an expert right away; you'll learn a lot more about working with collections in Chapter 2.

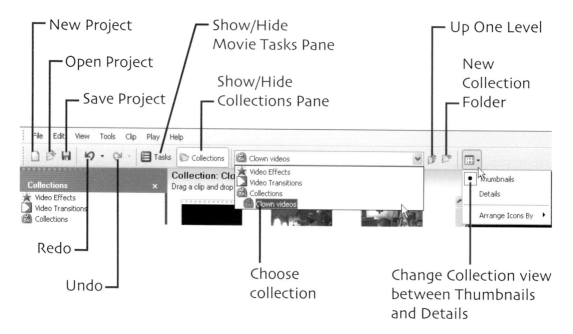

New Project

Open Project

Save Project

Show/Hide Movie Tasks Pane

Show/Hide Collections Pane

Up One Level

New Collection Folder

Redo

Undo

Choose collection

Change Collection view between Thumbnails and Details

welcome to movie maker

resize the work area

You can resize Movie Maker's windows to suit your needs. Simply hover the pointer over any solid blue line until the pointer changes to a two-headed arrow. Click and then drag the line until that window is sized to your liking. You can use this feature to maximize the size of whatever window you're working in. If you think Whatley's smiling now, wait until she watches this movie I'm making!

set project options

Choose Tools > Options to access Movie Maker's project default options.

Most of these options are self-explanatory, but a few bear some comment.

For convenience, store your content and project files in the same folder. That way, you can always find the files to use them again, and you can easily delete them when the project is complete. I usually create the folder on my capture drive, which is a separate disk drive used solely for video editing. Even on my laptop, which has only one drive, I always create a separate folder for each project.

Select the Save Auto-Recover option to have Movie Maker save your project file automatically so if your computer crashes, you won't lose all of your work. Try a setting of 10 minutes. No matter what autorecover setting you use, also save your project frequently, just to be safe.

Codecs are the compression technologies used to render and output your project. It's a good idea to keep them current, so keep this option checked.

You'll use passwords in Chapter 10 when uploading files to the Web. If multiple users access your computer and you're concerned that they may upload files to your Web site, here's an easy way to delete your passwords.

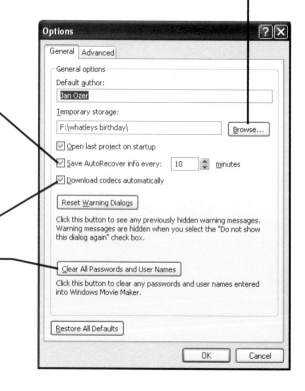

welcome to movie maker

Click the Advanced tab to access these functions.

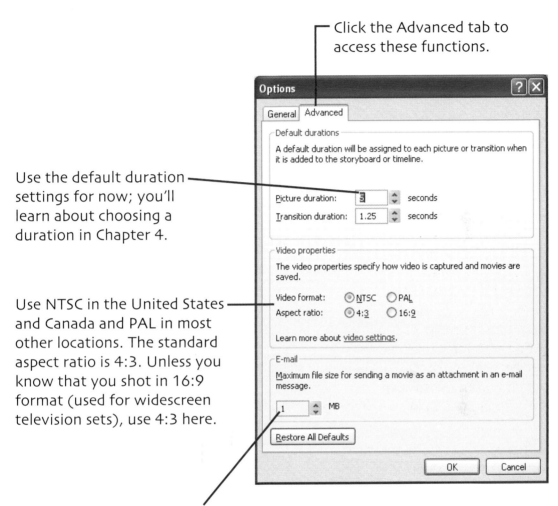

Use the default duration settings for now; you'll learn about choosing a duration in Chapter 4.

Use NTSC in the United States and Canada and PAL in most other locations. The standard aspect ratio is 4:3. Unless you know that you shot in 16:9 format (used for widescreen television sets), use 4:3 here.

Movie Maker automatically limits the size of videos produced for e-mail distribution to the size set here. Check with your Internet service provider (ISP) to learn what your sending limit is, and recognize that most recipients have a receiving limit as well. For example, my Hotmail account limits these attachments to 1 MB. Be sure to consider both your limits and your recipients' when setting this default. If you don't know the limits set by your ISP or those of your recipient, use 1 MB.

extra bits

movie maker tour p. 2

- This book describes Movie Maker 2, which is available for free download at http://www. microsoft.com/windowsxp/ moviemaker/|downloads/ moviemaker2.asp.

set project options p. 6

- Changing the Picture Duration setting affects pictures and transitions inserted after you make the change (not those previously inserted into the project).

welcome to movie maker

2. collecting project assets

I like collecting all of my audio and video clips and pictures—the project assets, or content—before I start serious editing, and that's what you'll do here. You'll set up and capture—or transfer—some video from a DV camera and import some audio files and still pictures, such as those shot with a digital camera. You'll also learn to manage these collections in Movie Maker's Collections pane.

I'm assuming that you've already shot your video and that you may have some digital photographs and music files already stored on your computer that you want to use to create a slide show to include with your video footage. You'll be getting these assets into Movie Maker in this chapter and then working with them to create your project in the rest of this book.

Here's a collection of digital pictures.

Movie Maker 2 stores all content in Collections located here. ——

You can build movies from video and digital pictures and add your own background music tracks or narration.

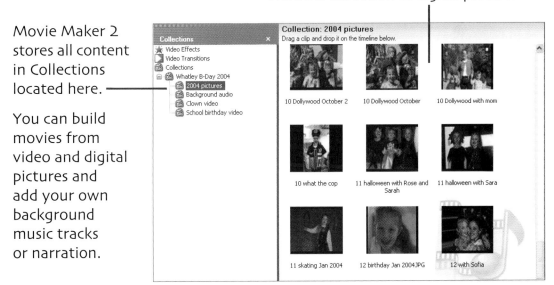

set up for dv capture

Find the DV output port on your DV camera. It's usually marked DV, as shown here.

Not this one—it's for analog audio-video you watch on your TV.

Not this one—LANC is a little-used standard for controlling your camera with external devices.

Not this one—it's the universal serial bus (USB) port used to send still pictures to the computer.

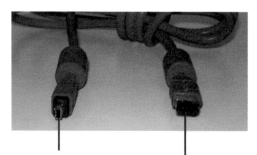

4-pin to 6-pin DV cable. This end goes into your camera.

This end goes into the DV card in your computer. Note that some laptops have 4-pin ports, like the DV camera shown here, instead of 6-pin ports. If this is the case for your computer, make sure you buy a 4-pin to 4-pin DV cable.

6-pin FireWire port on the computer. You can connect the cable to any FireWire port on the bracket.

Power up your camera and set it to VTR or Play mode.

capture dv

1 With your video camera connected to your computer, click here to start the capture process. If the Movie Tasks pane isn't visible, click the Show Movie Tasks Pane button on the main toolbar.

2 Click the Browse button to choose a folder for the captured video and enter a file name. Click Next at the bottom of the screen to continue (not shown).

3 The best approach is to work in DV-AVI format since that's the highest-quality format. You can always render your final movie in a different format, as you'll see in Chapter 10.

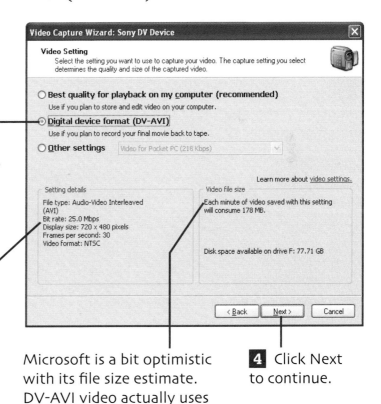

These are the parameters for the captured video. There's nothing here you really need to know about at this point. You'll learn a bit more about these in Chapter 10.

Microsoft is a bit optimistic with its file size estimate. DV-AVI video actually uses 216 MB per second.

4 Click Next to continue.

collecting project assets

capture dv (cont.)

Capture Method

Select whether to capture the entire tape automatically or specific parts manually.

○ **Capture the entire tape automatically**

The video tape rewinds to the beginning and the video is then captured automatically.

◉ **Capture parts of the tape manually**

Cue the video tape to the part of the video you want to capture and start the capture process manually. You can capture more than one part of the video tape without restarting the wizard.

☑ **Show preview during capture**

On some computers, displaying the Preview window during the video capture can affect the quality of the captured video. If you find that your captured video files do not play back smoothly, clear this checkbox.

5 Capturing the entire tape is easy—just select the top option and on the next screen click Start Capture. But often, you'll want to capture-only a portion of the tape for your video. You'll do this here. To start, select Capture Parts of the Tape Manually.

If you're working on a slow computer (Pentium III or slower), I recommend that you uncheck the Show Preview During Capture check box, which lets the computer concentrate solely on capturing the video. Most modern computers are fast enough to capture and show the preview at the same time.

6 Click Next to continue (not shown).

7 Watch the preview window and use these player controls to move the tape to the desired start position and then stop the tape.

8 Click Start Capture, and Movie Maker will start the tape rolling and start capturing. The Stop Capture button becomes active; click it if you want to stop capturing. Repeat step 7 and this step until you've captured all necessary video.

Select the Create Clips check box to have Movie Maker create a separate clip for each time you started and stopped the camera during shooting. This can be a real time saver, especially when you shot the tape over a few days or longer, since it breaks the video into the scenes as you shot them. Otherwise, Movie Maker will show just one clip in the Contents pane, and you'll have to identify the scenes yourself.

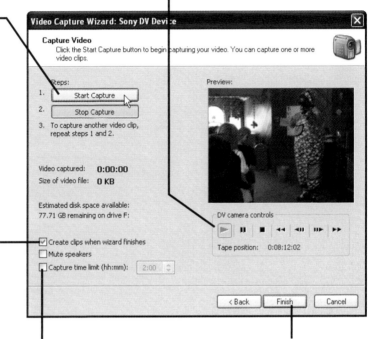

You can set the capture time limit to capture a specific duration of tape (for instance, the last 20 minutes of a tape). Then you can walk away and let Movie Maker stop the capture for you.

9 Click Finish when you've finished capturing all your video clips.

collecting project assets

capture dv (cont.)

After you click Finish, if you checked Create Clips, Movie Maker scans the captured video for scene breaks (where you stopped and started the camera during shooting) and imports each scene into the collection as a separate video clip.

Note, however, that Movie Maker actually stores only one file on your hard disk for each capture session.

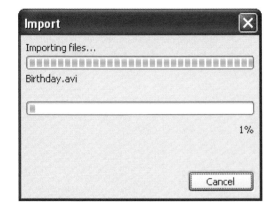

Movie Maker stores each capture session as a separate collection.

Click the collection name to display the collection in the Contents pane.

Movie Maker displays the captured video in the Contents pane. Double-click any thumbnail image, and Movie Maker will play the video in the Monitor.

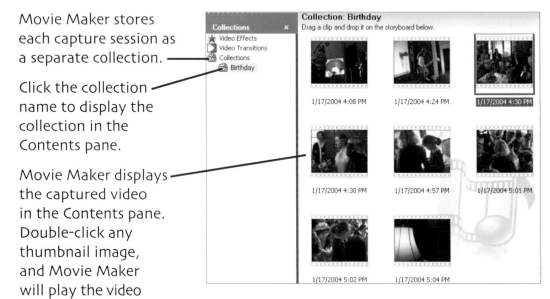

set up collections

Each time you capture or import video, Movie Maker stores it in a separate collection. In contrast, when you import digital pictures or audio, Movie Maker includes those files in the currently selected collection. I like to create one project collection, under which I store all other collections that contain video, audio, or still images. To keep my audio and still image assets separate, first I create a collection for each type, and then I import the assets into that collection. Start by creating your own project collection.

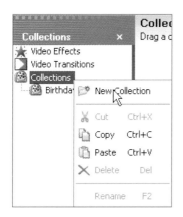

1 Click the Collections folder. Then right-click and choose New Collection.

Collections work like folders in Winows Explorer.

2 Here's your new collection. Type the desired name.

This descriptive name should make this collection easy to find. Now move all collections containing content for this project under the collection you just created.

set up collections (cont.)

3 To arrange your collections, simply drag them onto the target collection. When the target collection is highlighted, release the mouse, and Movie Maker will insert your dragged collection under the collection you selected. I dragged my collection under the Whatley B-Day 2004 collection.

4 Oops—calling the video collection Birthday was a bit too general. I need to change the name to something more specific. To change the name of a collection, click the collection; then right-click and choose Rename.

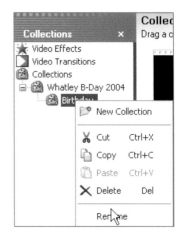

Enter a new name. Yes—Clown Video is much more descriptive.

5 Now add collections for your digital pictures and audio files, using the New Collection right-click menu option, as I did here. In a moment, you'll import those assets directly into these collections.

collecting project assets

import pictures

1 Click the collection in which you want to store your pictures.

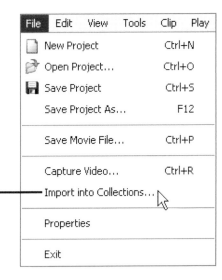

2 From the Movie Maker menu, choose File > Import into Collections.

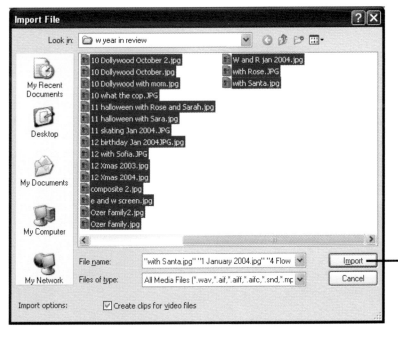

3 In the Import File dialog box that appears, navigate to the folder that contains your pictures and select all of the pictures you want to import.

4 Click Import.

import pictures (cont.)

Here are my pictures, perfect slide show material.

Click the collection name
in the Collections pane...

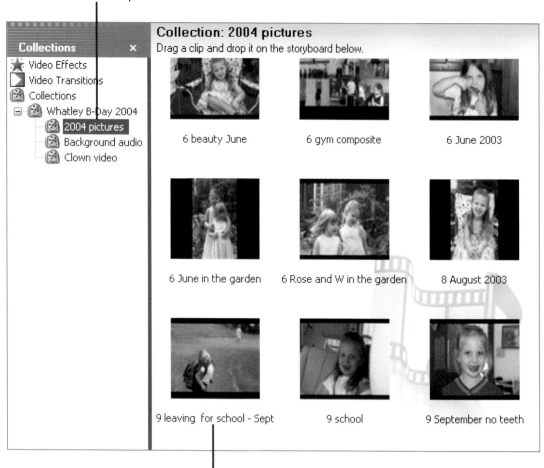

...to display the collection contents
in the Contents pane.

Click any image, and Movie Maker
will display it in the Monitor.

import audio

Importing music is very similar to importing pictures. You can use the Movie Maker menu as you did to import pictures. Or if you like working with the Movie Tasks pane open, you can choose your collection in the Collections drop-down box. You'll use that approach now.

1 Click the target collection.

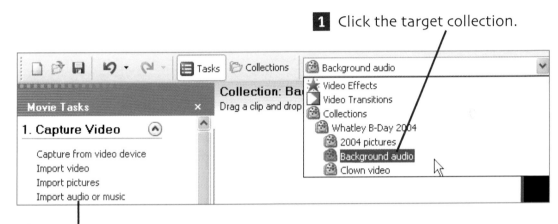

2 Click Import Audio or Music.

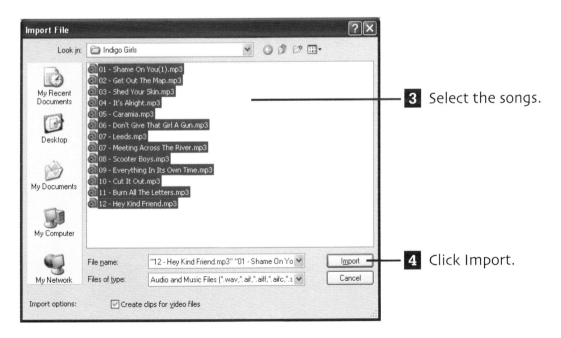

3 Select the songs.

4 Click Import.

import audio (cont.)

Click here to display the contents in Details view, to view the song name and duration.

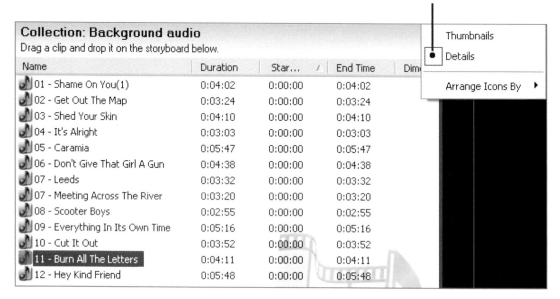

My wife loves the Indigo Girls, so they're a safe choice as background music for slide shows. As I've learned, Springsteen is a tough sell to mommy and the girlies, despite my singing the girlies to sleep with "Thunder Road" and "Jungleland" innumerable times during their infant years.

collecting project assets

import video

1 If your video footage is already on your computer, you need to import it. Click Import Video.

Movie Maker always inserts captured and imported video in a separate collection located below the Collections root folder, so don't bother to click the target collection first.

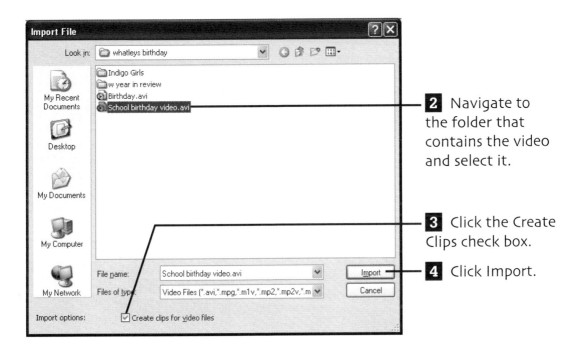

2 Navigate to the folder that contains the video and select it.

3 Click the Create Clips check box.

4 Click Import.

Because you selected Create Clips, Movie Maker breaks the video into separate clips at scene breaks, where you stopped and started the camera during shooting.

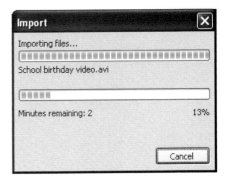

import video (cont.)

Here are the video clips, but the collection—in my case, School Birthday Video—is in the Collections root folder. Let's move it into the project folder—for me, the Whatley B-Day 2004 collection.

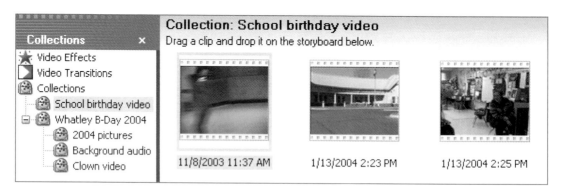

Collection: School birthday video
Drag a clip and drop it on the storyboard below.

11/8/2003 11:37 AM   1/13/2004 2:23 PM   1/13/2004 2:25 PM

Click, drag the collection down, and release.

Now all assets are right where they can easily be found. Time to start editing—head on to Chapter 3.

extra bits

set up collections p. 15

- Collections are not project specific. Once you create a collection in Movie Maker, it stays in the program until you delete it.
- To name each captured and imported video clip, Movie Maker inserts the time and date of the shot. This naming convention is a great feature when you have three months' worth of videos on a single tape, and you're trying to figure out when you shot each one. For instance, so when exactly did little Sally start walking? Just check the date!

import pictures p. 17

- Movie Maker can import .bmp, .dib, .gif, .jpeg, .jpg, .png, .tif, .tiff, and .wmf image formats.
- Movie Maker can't edit pictures after you import them, so if you need to rotate, remove red eye, or otherwise adjust your images, do so before importing.

import audio p. 19

- Movie Maker can import .aif, .aifc, .aiff, asf, .au, .mp2, .mp3, .mpa, .snd, .wav, and .wma audio files. The only noteworthy omission is files produced with RealNetworks technology, which usually have the .rn extension.

import video p. 21

- Movie Maker can import .asf, .avi, .m1v, .mp2, .mp2v, .mpe, .mpeg, .mpg, .mpv2, .wm, and .wmv video files.
- Movie Maker can't import QuickTime videos, with the .mov extension.

3. preparing your clips

When creating a birthday or other similar video, I try to accomplish two things. First, I try to tell a story, with a beginning, middle, and end. This helps keep the viewer's attention. Second, I try to chronicle the event, primarily by making sure I include all key shots inherent to the occasion, like a shot of everyone singing "Happy Birthday," and all key participants, typically family and important friends. Then I chop off the rest, aggressively and relentlessly, typically in the Contents pane, because it's a great place to isolate the key clips and delete the rest. When I'm done, I move to the Storyboard and Timeline to finish the work.

At this point, if you opted to allow Movie Maker to create clips as described in Chapter 2, you're probably staring at a bunch of video clips in the Contents pane: one for each time you started and stopped recording on your DV camera. Having these clips broken out is helpful, but to provide the necessary pace, you'll usually need to split these clips—that is, break the clips into smaller clips, each containing a shot you want to include in the final movie.

Movie Maker's Contents pane is a great place to identify the clips you'll include in your movie.

Isolating all the clips you'll include in your movie may be time consuming, but building the movie from these clips will now take no time at all.

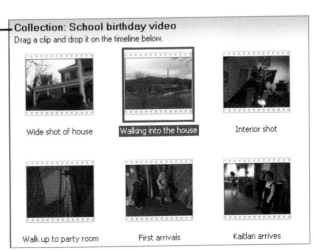

Collection: School birthday video
Drag a clip and drop it on the timeline below.

Wide shot of house   Walking into the house   Interior shot

Walk up to party room   First arrivals   Kaitlan arrives

delete video clips

Collection: School birthday video
Drag a clip and drop it on the timeline below.

11/8/2003 1

1/13/2004 2:25 PM

Add to Timeline	Ctrl+D
Play Clip	Spacebar
Cut	Ctrl+X
Copy	Ctrl+C
Paste	Ctrl+V
Delete	Del
Rename	F2
Create Clips	
Combine	Ctrl+M
Browse for Missing File...	
Properties	

1/13/2004 2

1/13/2004 2:36 PM

1/13/2004 2:40 PM

1/13/2004 2:44 PM

1/17/2004 2:11 PM

Begin by deleting unneeded clips in the Contents pane. For the birthday movie, the first clip I'll use is the one of my house. I'll delete all the clips before it.

1 Hold down the Shift key and select the clips you want to delete.

2 Right-click.

3 Choose Delete.

split clips

Next, split the clips—that is, break them into multiple clips—so each shot you later drag to the Timeline is a separate clip.

1 Click the clip that you want to split.

Movie Maker loads it into the Monitor.

2 Drag the Seek bar to a position a few seconds after a usable shot in the clip.

3 Click the Split the Clip button.

Movie Maker splits the clip into two clips, adding another clip to the Contents pane.

Initial clip, up to the split point.

New clip.

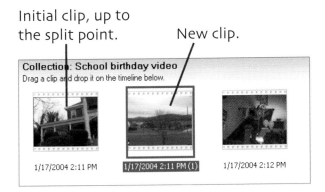

Continue to scroll through this and other clips in the Contents pane and split the clips as necessary.

rename clips

Now rename your clips so they're
easier to find when you're editing.

1 Click the clip
that you want to rename.

2 Right-click.

3 Choose Rename.

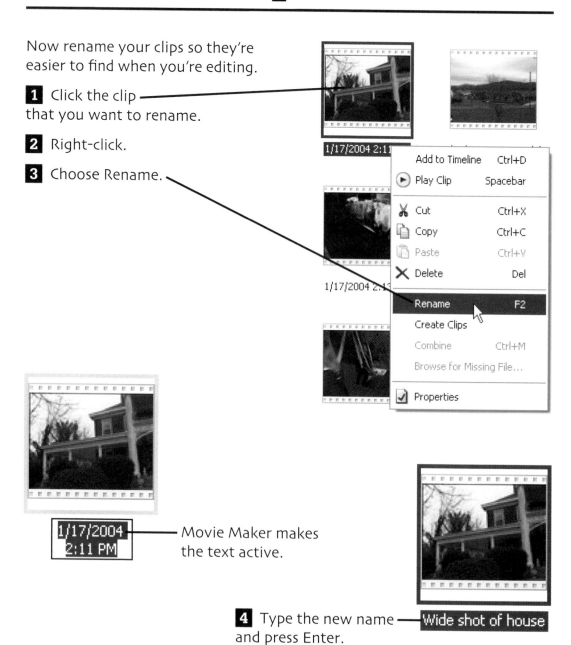

1/17/2004 2:11

Add to Timeline	Ctrl+D
▶ Play Clip	Spacebar
✄ Cut	Ctrl+X
📋 Copy	Ctrl+C
📋 Paste	Ctrl+V
✕ Delete	Del
Rename	F2
Create Clips	
Combine	Ctrl+M
Browse for Missing File...	
☑ Properties	

1/17/2004 2:1

1/17/2004
2:11 PM ——— Movie Maker makes
the text active.

4 Type the new name ——— Wide shot of house
and press Enter.

tell the story

Before you get too far in the splitting process, plan the visual flow of your movie to tell your story. Then use the procedures discussed earlier in this chapter—deleting, splitting, and renaming—to isolate the shots in the Contents pane. Here are the key shots I'll include in the birthday movie.

Wide shot of house

I start with a shot of the house—technically called an establishing shot, because it establishes the location in the viewer's mind.

Interior shot

Since the party is taking place indoors, I add an interior shot to provide more visual context.

First arrivals

Folks are coming! I try to find shots of all key friends and relatives as they arrive.

The gang's all here

Next come shots of pre-entertainment meeting and greeting (multiple shots of key guests).

Enter the clown

The clown arrives and performs.

Balloon fight 1

The entertainment concludes with balloon swords and helmets for all, creating general havoc (multiple clips of key guests).

tell the story (cont.)

Time for cake

That lasts until it's time for the cake. The crowd comes down the stairs.

Happy Birthday Son

Everyone sings "Happy Birthday."

Cake and food

Then everyone starts chowing down (multiple clips of key guests).

Finally! Presents

Finally it's time to open presents (multiple clips of key guests).

Parting is such swee

Then it's time for hugs and air kisses (multiple clips of key guests).

Now, with your key clips isolated, you're ready to move to the Storyboard and Timeline.

preparing your clips

extra bits

split clips p. 27

- To understand the process of splitting a clip, you need to understand the difference between a clip and a shot. Briefly, clip is the technical term used by Movie Maker to describe what's represented as a thumbnail in the Contents pane. In contrast, a shot is a segment of video within that clip that you may or may not want to use in the final movie. For example, when shooting at the party, I left the camera running for 2 or 3 minutes at a time. When Movie Maker creates clips, it will leave me with clips of that length. Within each clip are many shorter shots that I'll want to include in the movie—say 5 seconds here of one daughter, 6 seconds there of a friend, and 3 seconds of my other daughter. The only way for me to access these shots within Movie Maker is to isolate them each in a separate clip.

- When splitting clips in the Contents pane, don't worry about starting and stopping on the exact target frame. The editing tools in the Timeline are much more precise and efficient—you can make your final adjustments there. In fact, try to split clips a few seconds before the first frame you want to appear in the final movie and a few seconds after the last frame. This will give you flexibility if you want to fade into or out of the clip or insert a transition (see Chapter 5) before or after the clip.

- Some clips, like the Happy Birthday Song clip in my birthday video, will obviously have to be long enough to cover the entire event. Most other clips, however, such as those shot just to make sure that all relevant friends and family make it into the video, should be as short as possible, under 5 seconds if possible.

- Note that all these gyrations don't affect the files on your hard drive one bit; they remain totally unchanged.

extra bits (cont.)

tell the story p. 29

- Obviously, you can't include clips in your projects that you haven't first shot with your video camera. When I shoot an event, be it a wedding, concert, birthday, or family outing, I make a short list of required shots for that event before I leave for the shoot. It's typically pretty easy to formulate the list if you think about it in advance, but if you try to get all the shots without planning, you're bound to miss one or two.

preparing your clips

4. assembling your clips

So far, you've collected all your project assets—video, audio, and still images—and created and named all the clips to be included in the final project. In this chapter, you're going to drag everything to the Storyboard and/or Timeline, trim away unnecessary frames, create a slide show segment of the movie composed of digital pictures, and add background audio. In other words, you're building the movie. Sure, you'll be adding lots of polish in subsequent chapters, but that will only embellish the building blocks laid in this chapter.

You'll start here in Storyboard view, which is great for sequencing your clips.

Trimming your video clips into the shortest possible segments is the best way to keep your viewers interested in the content. Just click and drag.

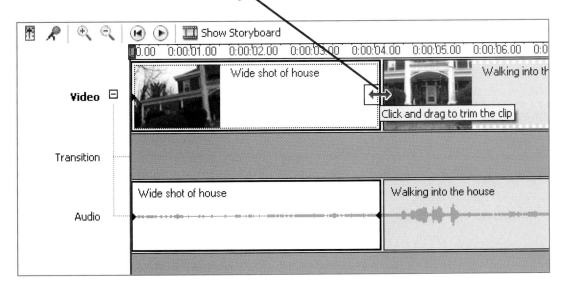

drag to storyboard

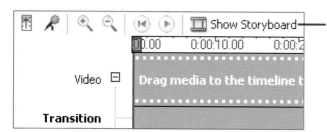

If you've worked with Movie Maker before, you may be in Timeline view. Click Show Storyboard at the top left of the Timeline to return to Storyboard view.

1 Click a clip in your collection to select the clip.

2 Hold down the mouse button and drag the clip to the first open frame on the Storyboard (you'll see a faint image of the thumbnail as you drag).

3 Release the mouse button. You've now added a clip to the Storyboard.

Movie Maker inserts the clip in the frame. Music Maker also drags down the audio portion of the video file, so you never have to worry about losing sound synchronization.

drag between clips

After you've dragged down some clips, you may want to add a clip between two clips.

1 Select a clip in your collection.

2 Hold down the mouse button and drag the clip to the desired location. The ghosted image shows where you are dragging the clip.

3 Release the mouse button.

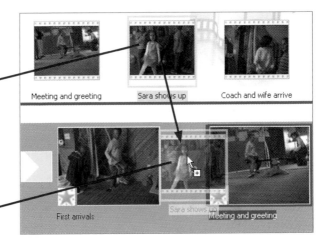

Meeting and greeting   Sara shows up   Coach and wife arrive

First arrivals   Sara shows up   Meeting and greeting

Here's the inserted clip.

First arrivals   Sara shows up   Meeting and greeting   Coach and wife arrive

Drag this slider bar in either direction to move around the Storyboard.

rearrange clips

Oh, goodness. That last screen reminded me that I want all arrival shots before the meeting and greeting shots—I need to move the Meeting and Greeting clip after the Coach and Wife Arrive clip. You can easily rearrange your clips on the Storyboard.

Meeting and greeting   Coach and wife arrive   Playing around

1 On the Storyboard, select the clip you want to move. I selected the Meeting and Greeting clip.

2 Hold down the mouse button and drag the clip where you want it. Watch for a vertical blue line to appear at the edge of the frame; Movie Maker will drop the clip in front of this frame.

3 Release the mouse button.

Coach and wife arrive   Meeting and greeting   Playing around

Movie Maker shifts the other clips to make room. For me, Movie Maker shifted the coach and his wife to the left.

Movie Maker moves the clip—in this case, the Meeting and Greeting clip.

assembling your clips

preview your movie

Play the movie to see how it's flowing so far.

1 Select the first clip you want to preview.

2 Use these buttons to control playback.

After Movie Maker finishes playing the clip you selected, it will automatically continue on to the next clip.

Note that you can also use the spacebar on your keyboard to start and pause playback—probably the most useful keyboard shortcut in the program.

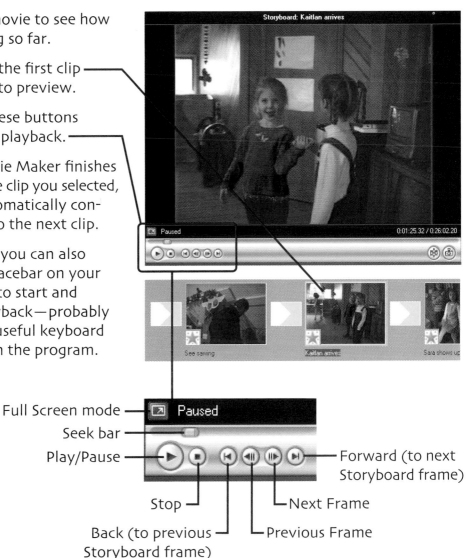

Full Screen mode
Seek bar
Play/Pause
Stop
Back (to previous Storyboard frame)
Previous Frame
Next Frame
Forward (to next Storyboard frame)

switch to timeline

After you've arranged your clips on the Storyboard, you can start trimming away unnecessary frames. To do so, you need to switch to Timeline view. Click Show Timeline.

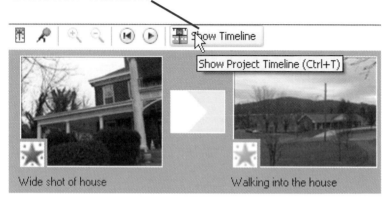

Wide shot of house | Walking into the house

Here's the Timeline, but with the Audio track hidden.

Click here to display the Audio track (you'll use it in Chapter 8).

Here's the Timeline in all its glory, with the Audio track displayed. It can look intimidating, but you'll find it easy to use once you get familiar with its tools and tracks.

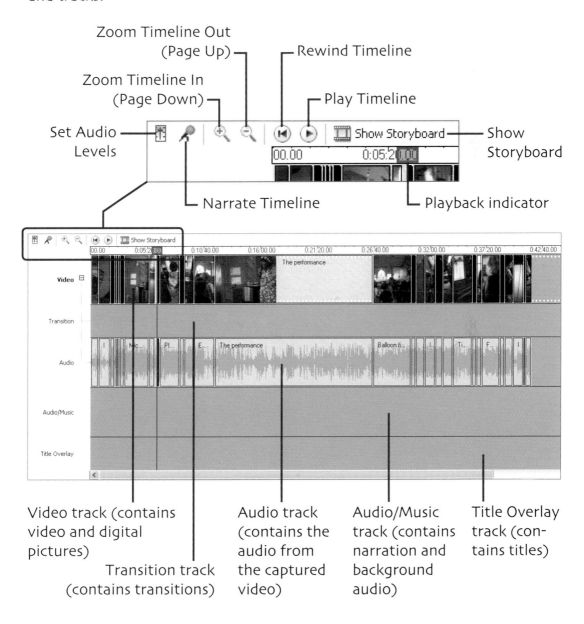

Video track (contains video and digital pictures)

Transition track (contains transitions)

Audio track (contains the audio from the captured video)

Audio/Music track (contains narration and background audio)

Title Overlay track (contains titles)

trim your clips

Trimming video is the process of removing unwanted frames from the beginning and end of your clips. The start trim point is the first frame that will play in your movie; the end trim point is the last frame.

You need to zoom in to trim a clip; click Zoom Timeline In until the target clip is clearly visible.

1 Click the clip.

2 Hover the mouse over the edge you want to trim until the trim cursor appears.

3 Click the mouse button.

4 If you're trimming away the beginning of a clip (as I am here), drag the left edge and watch the Monitor until the first frame you want to remain in the movie appears.

5 If you're trimming away the end of the clip, drag the right edge and watch the Monitor until the last frame you want to remain in the movie appears.

6 Release the mouse button.

Note that you can reverse the trim at any time by dragging the edge back out or by clicking the Undo button on the top toolbar.

assembling your clips

split your clips

You can also split a clip on the Timeline.

1 While watching the Monitor, drag the Playback indicator to where you want to split the clip.

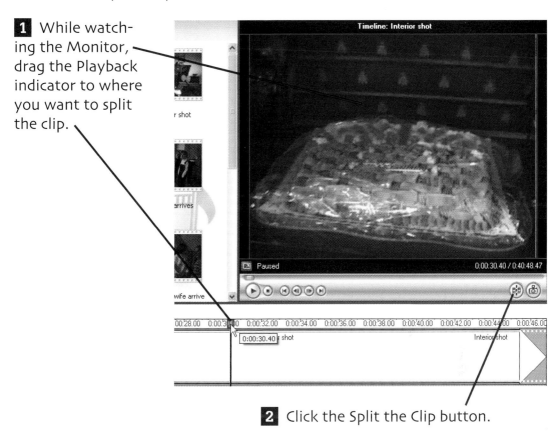

2 Click the Split the Clip button.

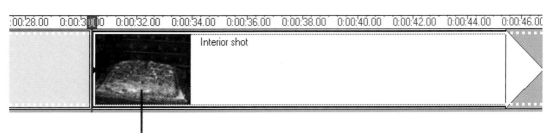

Movie Maker splits the clip, starting the new clip at the split location.

save your project

You've already put a lot of effort into your project, so it's time to save your work.

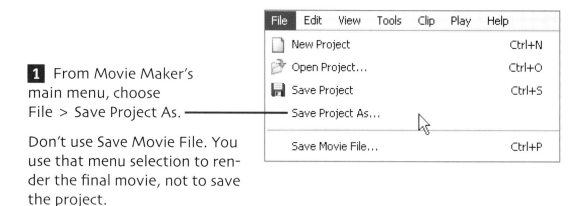

1 From Movie Maker's main menu, choose File > Save Project As.

Don't use Save Movie File. You use that menu selection to render the final movie, not to save the project.

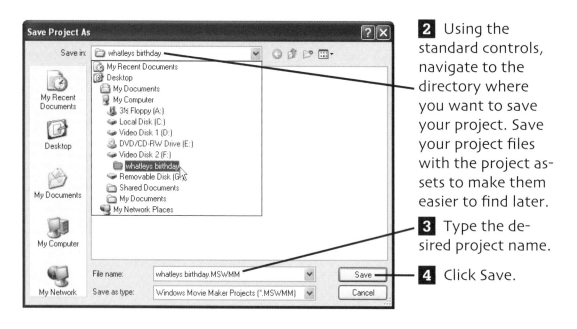

2 Using the standard controls, navigate to the directory where you want to save your project. Save your project files with the project assets to make them easier to find later.

3 Type the desired project name.

4 Click Save.

assembling your clips

insert pictures

Now you'll start the slide show component of the movie. Here you'll add digital pictures to the Timeline and then add background music; Movie Maker will convert this content to video when rendering the final movie. You'll be using the still pictures and a background audio file that you imported in Chapter 2. Then you'll add some transitions—visual effects that help smooth the move from one clip to the next, covered in detail in Chapter 5—between the slides. You'll start by checking the picture and transition duration settings.

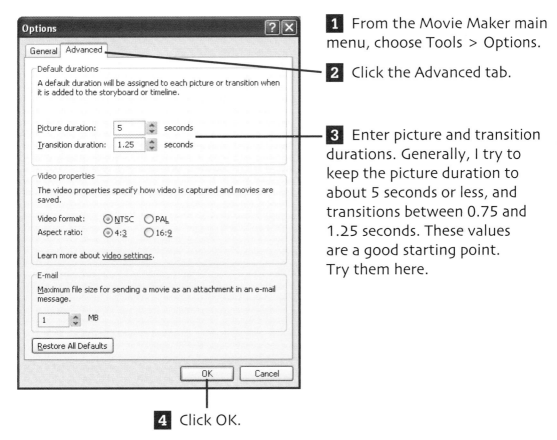

1 From the Movie Maker main menu, choose Tools > Options.

2 Click the Advanced tab.

3 Enter picture and transition durations. Generally, I try to keep the picture duration to about 5 seconds or less, and transitions between 0.75 and 1.25 seconds. These values are a good starting point. Try them here.

4 Click OK.

After applying these durations and inserting the background music clip, you'll check to see how closely the slide show and background music are synchronized.

create a slide show

Now add the pictures to the Timeline. You can insert them anywhere in the movie. For my project, I'm adding them to the end of the production, after all the trimmed video clips.

1 Click the collection that contains your pictures to open it in the Contents pane.

2 Click the Contents pane.

3 Right-click and choose Select All.

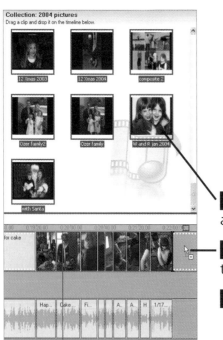

4 Click any picture in the Contents pane and hold down the mouse button.

5 Drag the picture to the Video track on the Timeline, after all of your video clips.

6 Release the mouse button.

insert music files

Your pictures are on the Video track. Now add the background audio. Select the audio collection so that the desired audio clip is showing in the Contents pane.

1 Select the audio clip in the Contents pane.

2 Hold down the mouse button and drag the audio clip to the Audio/Music track, so that the audio clip starts directly beneath the left edge of the first digital picture in the slide show.

3 Release the mouse button.

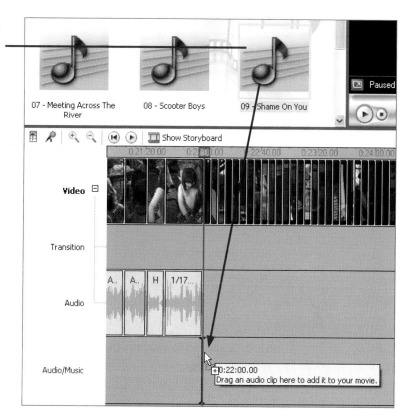

finish the slide show

Now check to see how closely the audio clip and slide show are synchronized by examining the Timeline after the audio has been inserted.

This audio clip is about 80 seconds shorter than the slide show.

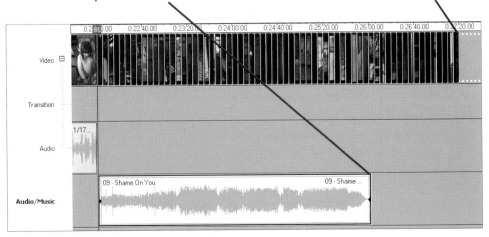

You'll need to slip in the transitions to check the final synchronization. (I'll teach you how in the next chapter. For now, just read on to see how the process works.)

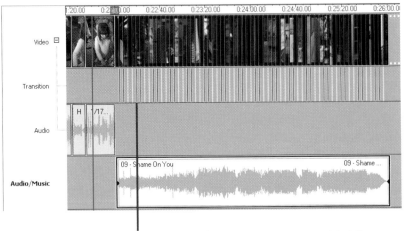

See all those little lines on the Transition track? Those are the transitions, and with them inserted, the two tracks align almost perfectly.

adjust picture duration

Zoom in to check the synchronization close up.

Not bad—the slides and audio match to within about 1 second.

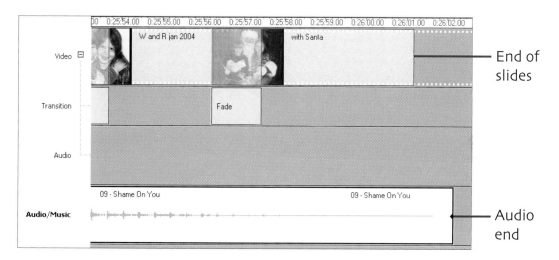

End of slides

Audio end

The final picture needs to be longer to make the synchronization exact.

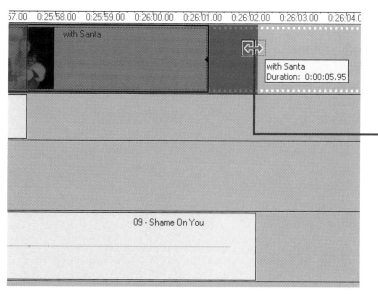

1 Click the picture.

2 Hover the mouse over the edge you want to trim until the trim cursor appears.

3 Click the mouse button and drag the edge to the desired position.

4 Release the mouse button.

extra bits

drag to storyboard p. 34

- If the video clips in the Contents pane are in the desired order, you can drag them all at once. Click the Contents pane and choose Edit > Select All from Movie Maker's main menu. Then drag the clips en masse to the Storyboard or Timeline. You can also hold down the Shift key to select contiguous clips, or Ctrl to select clips that aren't located next to each other.

- Many of the basic procedures shown in this chapter work identically in Timeline view, so if you prefer to work in Timeline view, use the same procedures.

save your project p. 42

- The project file doesn't contain the video, audio, and digital picture files that make up the project; it simply contains references to them. This keeps the project files small, but it means that you can't delete those files until after you've rendered your final movie.

- Deleting content from the Storyboard or Timeline does not delete it from your hard drive.

trim your clips p. 40

- In the next chapter, you'll learn about transitions, which are visual effects that help smooth the move from one clip to the next. If you plan to use transitions between clips, consider the transition duration when trimming your clips. For example, a 1-second fade transition creates a 1-second overlap between the two clips. When trimming, be sure that any critical action or audio in the first clip ends at least 1 second from the end of the clip, and that any critical action or audio in the second clip starts at least 1 second into that clip. Similarly, if you fade in from black (an effect discussed in Chapter 6), the first half-second of the clip will be partially obscured by the fade-in effect. When trimming, be sure that any critical action or audio starts after that half-second. Ditto at the end of a clip if you plan to fade to black at the clip's end.

assembling your clips

5. inserting transitions

Transitions are audio and visual effects used to smooth the flow from clip to clip. For example, in movies, you may have noticed the screen fade to black at the end of one scene and then fade back in at the start of the next. You may have also noticed that the audio followed suit, growing quieter during the fade to black and then welling up as the picture faded back in. These are transitions.

Note that you don't have to insert a transition between each clip in a project. If you don't insert a transition, the second clip starts playing immediately after the first clip ends, which is commonly called a cut transition.

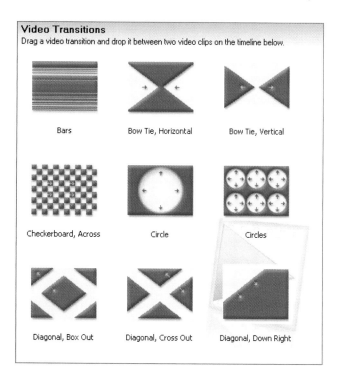

Movie Maker offers a good mix of transitions, and you can get more from Microsoft and third parties such as Pixelan.

Still, knowing which transitions to use, and when, is key to using transitions effectively.

explore transitions

1 In the Collections pane, click the Video Transitions collection to display Movie Maker's transitions in the Contents pane.

2 Double-click the transition you want to preview.

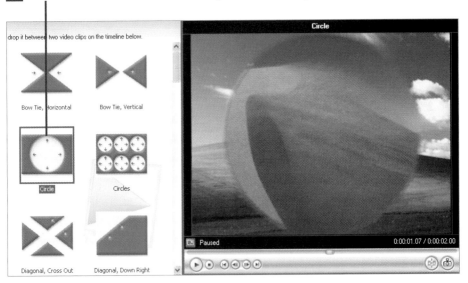

Movie Maker plays your selected transition in the Monitor.

For the Circle transition shown here, Microsoft supplies two images to help you preview the transition. The sunny hill and blue sky represent the first clip in the transition. The sand dune represents the second clip.

The Circle transition opens a widening circle in the first clip through which the second clip is visible.

Have some fun and preview any transitions that appeal to you.

insert a dissolve

I want to smooth the scene change from a view of the party room to the arrival of the first guests. This is a minor change, so I'll try a subtle dissolve transition, which blends frames from the two video clips with a touch of pixilation.

Find a similar spot in your project, where you're moving from one scene to another, making sure the change is equally minor. Working in either the Timeline or Storyboard view, have the intersection of the last clip from the first scene and the first clip from the second scene in view.

1 Display the Video Transitions collection in the Contents pane and select the Dissolve transition.

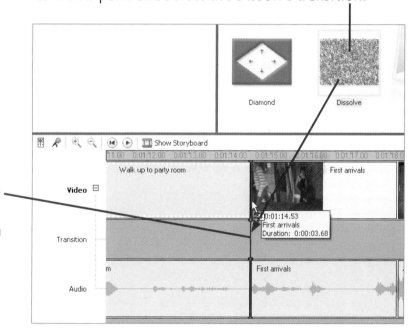

2 Hold down the mouse button and drag the transition to the intersection of the two clips.

3 Release the mouse button.

insert a dissolve (cont.)

Movie Maker inserts the transition on the Transition track.

This slightly opaque area (and the transition beneath it) represents the area of overlap between the two clips.

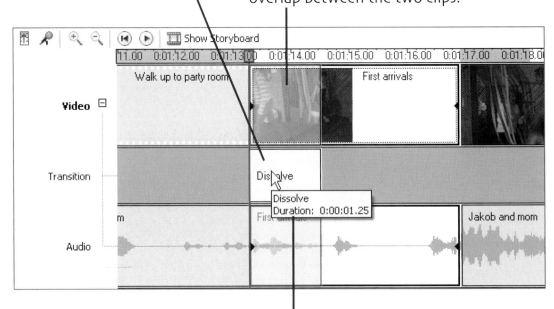

Note the information window Movie Maker displays when you hover your mouse over any content in the Timeline or Storyboard. You'll use this information in a moment to adjust the duration of the transition.

preview transitions

Now preview your transition to be sure it works like you want it to.

1 Double-click the transition in either the Time-line or Storyboard (shown).

2 Click the Play/Pause button (shown in Pause mode because the preview is playing).

When you preview your transition, Movie Maker plays it in the Monitor and then continues to play subsequent clips.

change transitions

The dissolve is pretty plain. My movie is a birthday party, so I think I should liven it up a bit. I'll try the Heart transition. See if this works for you.

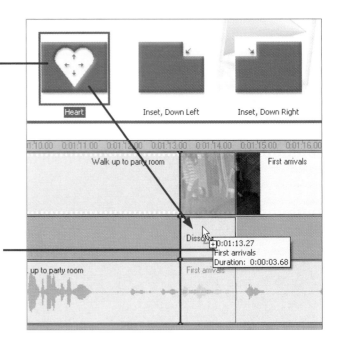

1 Select the new transition.

2 Hold down the mouse button and drag the transition to the previously inserted transition.

3 Release the mouse button.

When you replace a transition, the clip information window shows the data from the video clip above the transition, not the transition itself. Just ignore that and drop in the new transition.

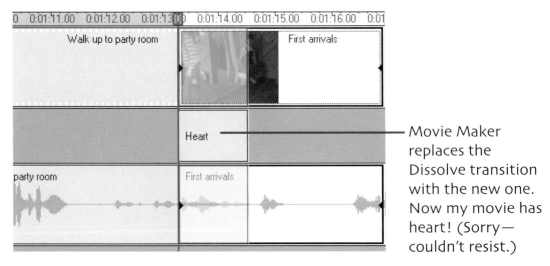

Movie Maker replaces the Dissolve transition with the new one. Now my movie has heart! (Sorry—couldn't resist.)

change duration

Preview your new transition. Mine flashes by a bit too quickly, so I'm going to make it longer. Two seconds sounds about right. Try a 2-second duration for your transition, too.

Be sure you're in Timeline view; you can't adjust the duration in Storyboard view.

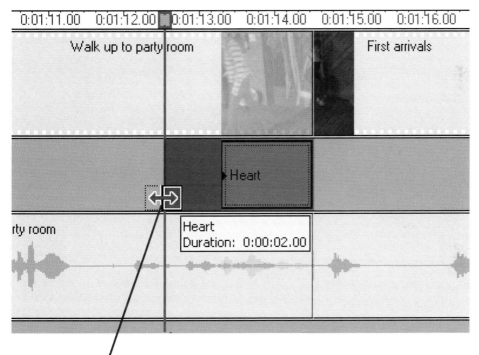

1 Hover the cursor over the left edge of the transition until the two-headed cursor appears.

2 Hold down the mouse button and drag the transition to the left, watching the information window until you've reached the target duration (2 seconds here).

3 Release the mouse.

Now preview again. With its longer duration, this transition looks a lot better.

fade audio out and in

You just inserted a video transition. Now you'll work on the audio. You'll fade out the audio on the clip before the transition—from 100% volume to 0%—and fade it back in on the clip after the transition—from 0% volume to 100%.

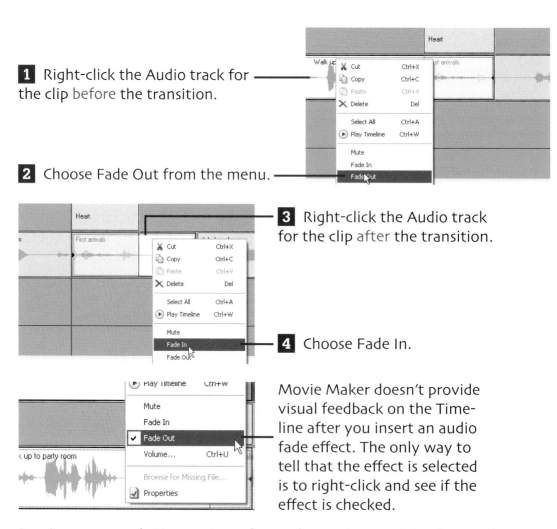

1 Right-click the Audio track for the clip before the transition.

2 Choose Fade Out from the menu.

3 Right-click the Audio track for the clip after the transition.

4 Choose Fade In.

Movie Maker doesn't provide visual feedback on the Timeline after you insert an audio fade effect. The only way to tell that the effect is selected is to right-click and see if the effect is checked.

Preview your work. You can't configure the settings, so it's take it or leave it, but if you don't like the way the fade sounds, delete it by following the same procedure: click the audio track, right-click, and choose the checked fade effect to remove the check mark.

fade video to black

Now move to the scene changes between the video portion of the project to the slide show. To let viewers know that a major change is occurring, you'll fade to black after the last video clip and then fade in from black to start the slide show.

1 Right-click the Video track of the target clip—here, the last video clip before the slide show.

2 Choose Fade Out.

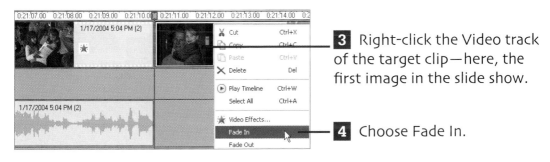

3 Right-click the Video track of the target clip—here, the first image in the slide show.

4 Choose Fade In.

To see if you've applied a fade effect, right-click the Video track and see if the option is checked.

repeat a transition

If you're building a slide show with 60 or so pictures, you'll be happy to learn that there's a way to insert the same transition between all of them at the same time. For this task, you need to work in Storyboard view.

Click Show Storyboard to change to Storyboard view, if necessary.

1 Click the first picture in the slide show.

2 Hold down the Shift key on your keyboard.

3 If necessary, drag this slider bar until you can see the last slide in the slide show.

4 Click the last picture in the slide show. All of your pictures should now be selected.

inserting transitions

5 In the Contents pane, right-click the desired transition. Try the Page Curl transition.

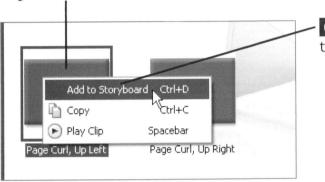

6 Choose Add to Storyboard.

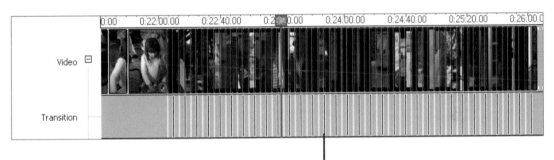

Switch to Timeline view. Each line on the Transition track is a transition that Movie Maker just inserted.

Important! Preview your work immediately to make sure that you like the transition you chose. If you don't, click Undo on the Movie Maker toolbar (at the upper left) and start over. Otherwise, if you change your mind later, you'll have to delete every single transition individually, which can be time consuming.

inserting transitions

extra bits

explore transitions p. 50

- How you use transitions is a matter of personal taste and style and should vary by the type of movie and the audience. The best way to learn how to use transitions is to pay attention to how they're used in movies and television. Serious movies and television shows usually stick to cuts, dissolves, and fades, while children's shows and comedies may use more obvious and fun transitions.

- I follow three rules when using transitions with video clips. First, I use transitions to alert the viewer to a change in scene or time, but only if I don't have video that does a better job than the transition. Second, I try to match the extent of the scene change and the transition. If it's a minor scene change, I use a modest, barely noticeable transition. If it's a major scene change, I use an obvious transition. And third, whenever I insert a video transition, I transition the audio as well, fading out the audio from the first clip and fading in the audio from the next clip.

- Slides shows are a bit of a different animal. I almost always use transitions between the slides.

- Remember that transitions overlap frames from the two affected video clips, partially obscuring the content for the duration of the transition. If you have important content at the start of the second clip or end of the first clip, make sure the transition doesn't obscure it. If it does, retrim the clip, adding the duration of the transition to the front or back of the clip, as necessary, to ensure that the transition doesn't obscure the content you want to appear.

inserting transitions

- Microsoft offers several sources of additional transitions, some free, some with a modest charge. You can download the free Windows Movie Maker 2 Winter Fun Pack 2003, which includes both a Snow Wipe and Snow Burst transition, at http://www.microsoft.com/ windowsxp/moviemaker/ downloads/winterfun.asp.

- Also consider the Microsoft Plus! Digital Media Edition, which costs $19.95 and can be found at http://www.microsoft. com/windows/plus/PlusHome. asp. The Plus! pack includes a range of useful transitions as well as other tools and effects.

- If you're serious about your transitions, surf over to http:// www.pixelan.com/mm/intro. htm. There, you'll find transitions and effects that extend Movie Maker's capabilities immensely.

change duration p. 55

- Each audio fade (in and out) lasts two-thirds of a second; you can't adjust the duration.

- All video fades (in and out) last half a second; you can't adjust the duration. There are techniques you can use to produce longer fades, but they're beyond the scope of this book. See Microsoft Windows Movie Maker 2: Visual QuickStart Guide from Peachpit Press for more details.

inserting transitions

6. applying special effects

Special effects are filters that change the appearance of video either to fix underlying problems or to enhance the video artistically. In both roles, they can help make your video much more watchable.

For example, if your video is too dark, perhaps because the lighting was inadequate during shooting, you can use effects to brighten it up before your viewers see it. In addition, you can use artistic special effects to change the pace and appearance of your video to help retain the viewer's interest.

Make no mistake, however; overusing special effects will likely have the reverse impact, like throwing too many different spices into a casserole. However, as you'll see, a dash here and a pinch there really helps make your movie more palatable to your viewers.

Use Movie Maker's Video Effects collection to cure problems with your video such as shots that are too bright or too dark.

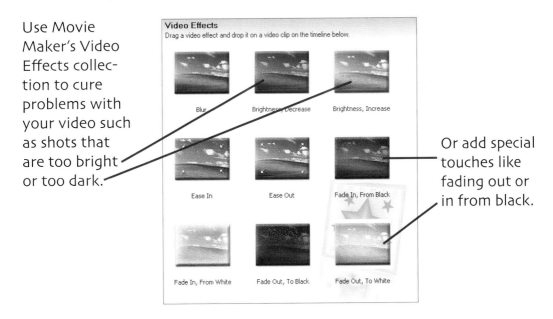

Or add special touches like fading out or in from black.

explore effects

Let's start by seeing where effects live in Movie Maker and how to preview them. You can apply effects to digital pictures as well as videos.

1 Click the Video Effects collection to display Movie Maker's effects in the Contents pane.

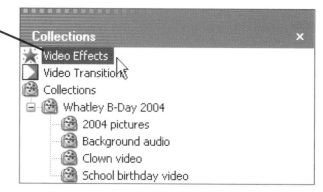

2 Double-click any effect...

...and Movie Maker previews it in the Monitor.

fade video in and out

I like to begin by fading in from black at the start of a movie. I'm working in Timeline view, but you can perform the same operations in Storyboard view.

1 Open the Video Effects collection in the Contents pane and select the Fade In, From Black effect.

2 Hold down the mouse button and drag the effect to the first clip on the Timeline.

3 Release the mouse button.

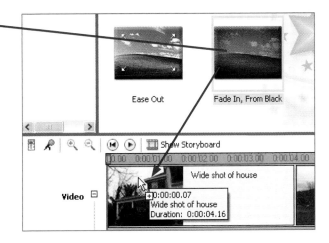

This star lets you know that you've applied an effect to the clip.

Now apply the Fade Out, To Black effect to the last clip in your project.

1 Select the Fade Out, To Black effect.

2 Hold down the mouse button and drag the effect to the last clip on the Timeline.

3 Release the mouse button.

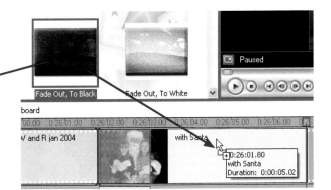

applying special effects

brighten a video clip

Truth be told, my daughter's birthday was a gray, dreary day, with a constant threat of snow. To create the appropriate birthday party atmosphere, I'm going to brighten my video a bit and then add some man-made snow to the mix. If you have any video that looks a bit too dark, try this effect on it. Or if you have a video that's a touch too bright, follow the same instructions but apply the Brightness, Decrease effect.

1 From the Video Effects collection, select the Brightness, Increase effect.

2 Hold down the mouse button and drag the effect to the target clip on the Timeline (in my project, I'm brightening the first two clips, the only two shot outdoors).

3 Release the mouse button. The effect is applied.

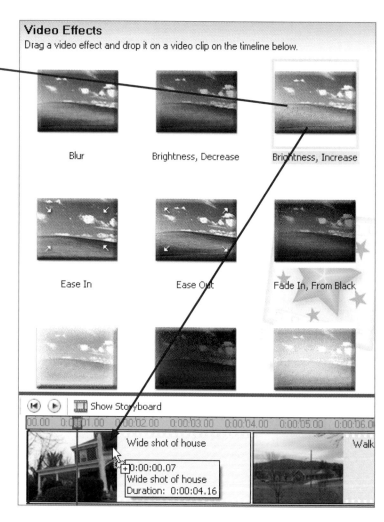

preview effects

Click Play on the Monitor to preview your effects to make sure they're producing the results you desire. Looks bright enough to me, but if you need to make your video even brighter, just drag the same Brightness, Increase filter down onto the clip one more time. All Movie Maker effects work this way: to increase the effect, drag it onto the clip again.

Now, if you like, try the Snowflakes effect, which comes with the free Movie Maker 2 Winter Fun Pack 2003 discussed in the "Extra Bits" sections of this chapter and Chapter 5.

1 From the Video Effects collection, select the Snowflakes effect.

2 Hold down the mouse button and drag the effect to the target clip on the Timeline.

3 Release the mouse button.

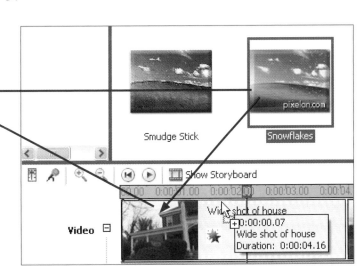

preview effects (cont.)

Timeline: Wide shot of house

Paused

0:00:02.27 / 0:26:09.00

Click Play to preview again. What do you think? Well, it probably won't fool my daughter into thinking that it snowed, but it just might make her laugh. Okay, giggle. Definitely smile. Leave it in or take it out? I'm going to leave it in (at least for now), but if I were going to remove it, here's how I would do it.

remove an effect

Okay; you applied an effect, but now you're having second thoughts. Here's how to remove the effect.

1 Right-click the Video track of the clip with the effect that you want to delete.

2 Choose Video Effects.

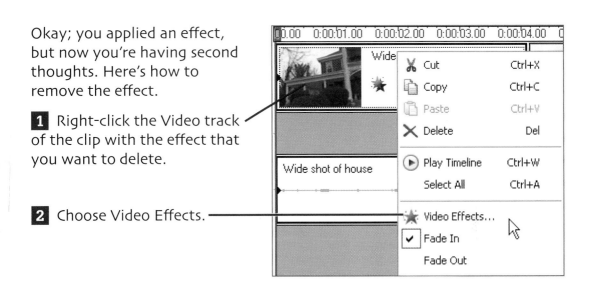

Movie Maker opens the Add or Remove Video Effects dialog box. Note that my clip has three effects applied; you can apply up to five effects to a clip.

3 In the Displayed Effects pane, select the effect that you want to delete.

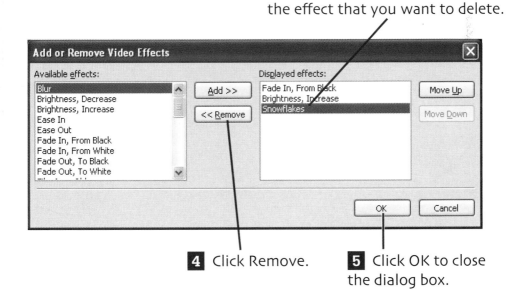

4 Click Remove.

5 Click OK to close the dialog box.

change playback speed

I use this effect a lot, generally to increase playback speed, but sometimes to slow it down as well. In my movie, I have a sequence of guests walking down the stairs to eat that was just begging to be speeded up, since folks walking at double speed (especially to eat cake) generally looks pretty funny. Find a sequence in your movie where there's a lot of action and try the same thing. When you preview, the audio will probably sound funny as well, as audio does when speeded up or slowed down, but you'll learn how to mute a clip in Chapter 8.

1 From the Video Effects collection, select the Speed Up, Double effect.

2 Hold down the mouse button and drag the effect to the target clip.

3 Release the mouse button.

Note that if you want to double the speed again, you just drag the effect down onto the clip again.

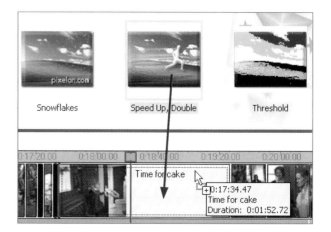

applying special effects

add motion to images

One of Movie Maker's strongest features is the capability that lets you add motion to still images. You have two options: the Ease In effect, which zooms into the picture, making it larger, and the Ease Out effect, which starts zoomed in and then zooms out. If you're using digital pictures in your project, such as those used for the slide show, try adding motion to them.

You can also apply both motion effects to video clips. The Ease In effect works particularly well when a clip holds steady on a single person, giving the impression that you zoomed in or out with your camcorder's zoom controls.

1 From the Video Effects collection, select the Ease In effect.

2 Hold down the mouse button and drag the effect to the target clip.

3 Release the mouse button.

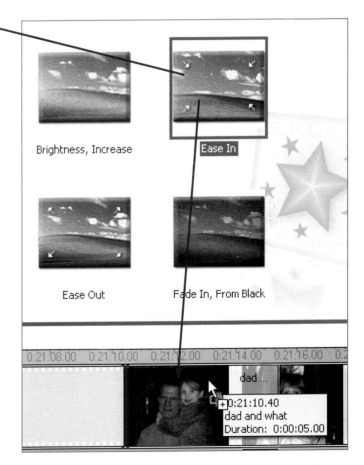

Brightness, Increase

Ease In

Ease Out

Fade In, From Black

0:21:08.00   0:21:10.00   0:21:12.00   0:21:14.00   0:21:16.00   0:2

dad ...

0:21:10.40
dad and what
Duration: 0:00:05.00

add motion to images

With the Ease In effect applied, the video starts here…

…and slowly zooms in to here over the duration of the video clip or picture. Note that I had to apply the effect several times to achieve this level of zoom.

extra bits

explore effects p. 64

- The special effects you choose should vary by video content. For example, though I adore Movie Maker's film age effects, which make a movie look like an old black-and-white film, they're tough to use in a video documenting a six-year-old's birthday party. That said, the effects I use in this project represent a core group that seem to find their way into most movies that I create.

- You can apply up to five effects to any video or picture on the Video track.

- The Snowflakes effect used in this chapter comes in the free Windows Movie Maker 2 Winter Fun Pack 2003, which you can download from http://www.microsoft.com/windowsxp/moviemaker/downloads/winterfun.asp. When you install this package, the effects will be added to your Video Effects collection.

- Pixelan takes Movie Maker's special effects to a different level, with effects that can adjust the color of your videos as well as provide many more motion options for your still images. You can choose from a variety of effects packages, each available for less than $20, at http://www.pixelan.com/mm/intro.htm.

fade video in and out p. 65

- To paraphrase Gertrude Stein, a fade is a fade is a fade. In the preceding chapter, you used fades between video clips as transitions; in this chapter, you applied them at the beginning and end of video clips as effects. You can insert fades the same way you did in the preceding chapter, via right-click commands, or by working through the special effects collection as you did here. Either way, they're the same effects, just used in different places.

extra bits (cont.)

change playback speed p. 70

- As you probably observed, when Movie Maker adjusts video speed, it also adjusts audio playback speed, which usually makes your audio un-usable. Generally, I mute the Audio track (turn down the volume to 0%) and add back-ground music on the Audio/ Music track that matches the speed change: slow and lugubrious for slow motion, fast and snappy for fast motion. More on this in Chapter 8.

add motion to images p. 71

- The Ease In and Ease Out effects are great for adding motion to still pictures, but the look can get repetitive. I typically apply this effect on every third or fourth image, usually switching between the two effects.

7. creating titles

Titles are text-based frames that can appear full screen on the Video track or superimposed over video clips or digital pictures. I generally use titles in at least three places in my video productions.

First, I open each movie with a title so the viewer knows what he or she will be watching. I also usually insert titles at scene changes, primarily to let the viewer know what's coming and that the movie is, in fact, moving along. Finally, I close most projects with closing credits.

Movie Maker's titles have two components: text and animation scheme. Movie Maker gives you great control over font, text color, size, positioning, and transparency. In addition, Movie Maker's title animation schemes let you control how titles move on and off screen and other visual characteristics you'll learn about in this chapter.

There's nothing like a great title to begin a movie.

You can control text font and colors.

You can also choose a title animation scheme, which controls the background and the way the title appears and disappears from the screen.

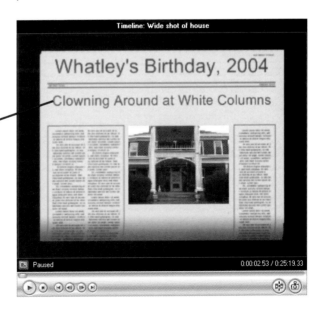

add an opening title

You'll begin by adding an opening title to your movie.

Although you can insert titles and credits in Storyboard view, I typically work almost exclusively in Timeline view by this stage in a project, so that's the view you'll use in this chapter.

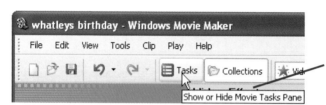

1 Since you've been working with effects, you probably have the Collections pane open. Click this button to open the Movie Tasks pane.

2 Click Make Titles or Credits.

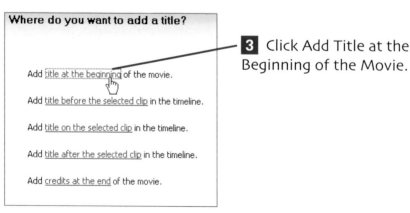

3 Click Add Title at the Beginning of the Movie.

creating titles

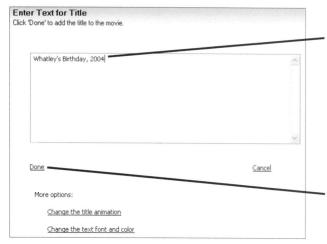

4 Type the desired text.

Note that the title I'm creating has only one text entry field, though your title may show two fields. More on this in a moment.

5 Click Done.

Movie Maker inserts the title at the start of the Video track. If you haven't yet adjusted the font, color, and animation options, Movie Maker uses the default settings; if you have, it uses the last settings that you applied. You'll learn how to change these settings in a bit.

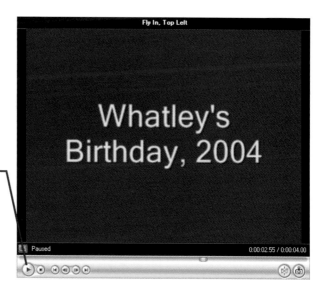

Click the Play button to see the title in the Monitor. Kind of plain—it might work for a serious movie, but it doesn't cut it for a six-year-old's birthday party. Let's try something else.

change to title overlay

You just produced a full screen title that uses a solid blue frame as background and sits on the Video track. You'll now change to an overlay title that sits in the Title Overlay track and appears over a video or digital picture.

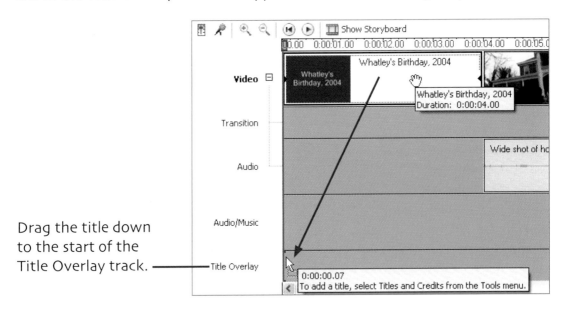

Drag the title down to the start of the Title Overlay track. ———

Movie Maker moves the first video clip to the left to fill the gap formerly occupied by the title.

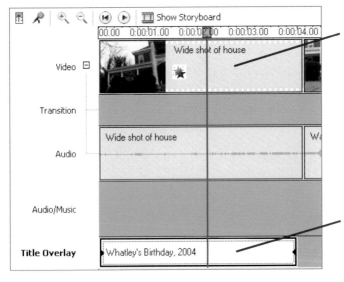

The title is now directly below the video clip. Preview to see what that looks like.

Better, but the white text from the title is hard to see against the white background. You may not have the same problem, but I definitely need to make this text more visible. Let's take a quick look at the options.

change title animation

I could change the font color, but perhaps a different title animation would produce a better result. In Movie Maker, title animations not only animate the text, but also insert different backgrounds, banners, and special effects, which may make the text more visible.

1 Double-click the title to open Movie Maker's title controls.

2 Click Change the Title Animation.

3 Select a different title animation.

Use this scrollbar to see all of your choices, which includes three groups of animations under separate headings: one-line and two-line titles and credits (which go at the end of the movie).

Click any animation scheme, and Movie Maker will display it in the Monitor. The Newspaper title animation is one of my favorites, so select that one.

4 Click Done.

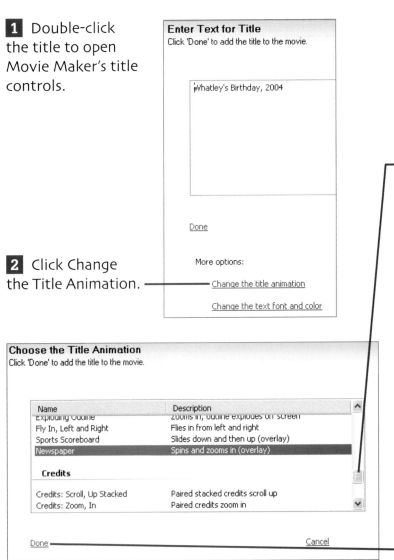

Enter Text for Title
Click 'Done' to add the title to the movie.

Whatley's Birthday, 2004

Done

More options:

Change the title animation

Change the text font and color

Choose the Title Animation
Click 'Done' to add the title to the movie.

Name	Description
Exploding Outline	Zooms in, outline explodes on screen
Fly In, Left and Right	Flies in from left and right
Sports Scoreboard	Slides down and then up (overlay)
Newspaper	Spins and zooms in (overlay)
Credits	
Credits: Scroll, Up Stacked	Paired stacked credits scroll up
Credits: Zoom, In	Paired credits zoom in

Done   Cancel

Here's the Newspaper title animation. However, it looks like there's room for another line of text. That's because this is a two-line title, and the title I created originally was a one-line title.

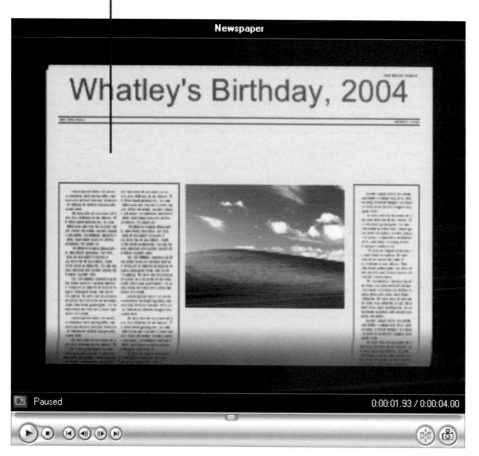

edit title text

Often, you'll have to edit the text of your title, perhaps to correct a misspelling. Or if you start with a one-line title animation and then choose a two-line title animation, as I did here, you may have room for another line of text.

1 Double-click the title to open the Enter Text for Title screen.

Now there are two lines for text where before there was only one.

2 Type the desired text.

3 Click Done.

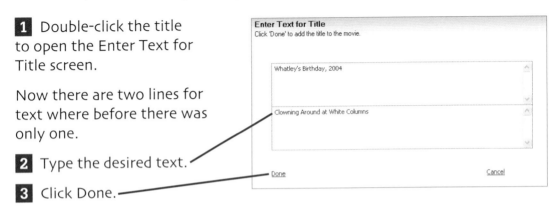

4 Preview your title.

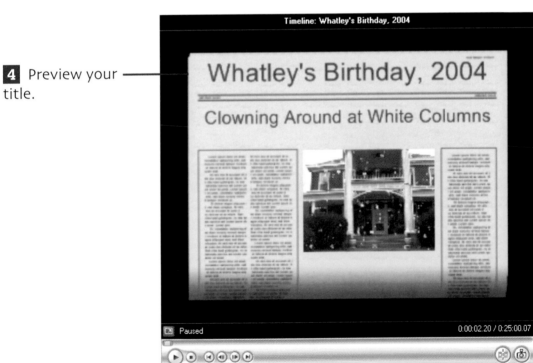

adjust title duration

So viewers have time to appreciate your title, you can make it stay on the screen longer than the 4-second default title duration.

1 Click the title.

2 Hover the mouse over the right edge until the trim cursor appears.

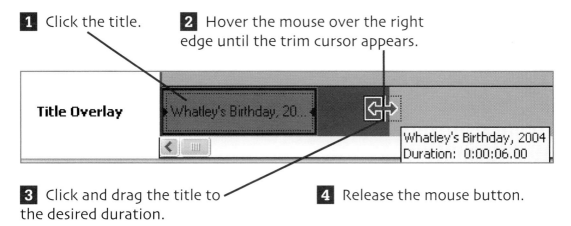

3 Click and drag the title to the desired duration.

4 Release the mouse button.

add title at new scene

The opening title is done. Now you'll add some titles at scene changes. These tell the viewers what's coming and lets them know that the movie is moving along, which helps minimize the fidgets.

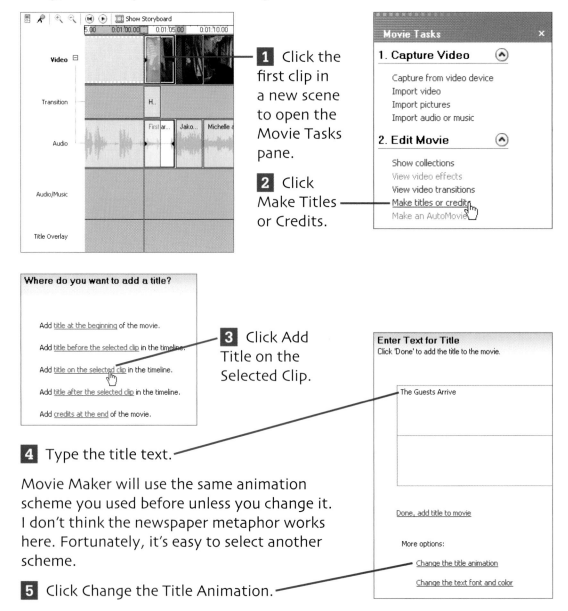

1 Click the first clip in a new scene to open the Movie Tasks pane.

2 Click Make Titles or Credits.

3 Click Add Title on the Selected Clip.

4 Type the title text.

Movie Maker will use the same animation scheme you used before unless you change it. I don't think the newspaper metaphor works here. Fortunately, it's easy to select another scheme.

5 Click Change the Title Animation.

creating titles

6 Choose a different animation scheme, such as this one-line News Banner title animation.

Note that titles with overlay in the name insert the text over a solid-colored background, making the text more readable. I use them almost exclusively.

7 Click Done.

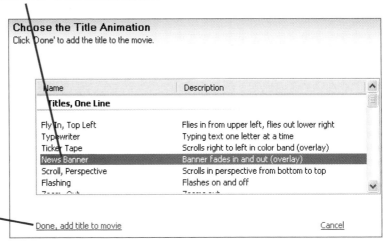

Here's the title. ——

view font controls

I like my text font to match the subject of my movies—elegant for holidays, fun for birthday parties, and so on. The title I just added doesn't quite fit the feel, so I'm going hunting for a font that screams six-year-old's birthday party.

All computers have different fonts that get loaded when you install different programs, so you may not have the font that I select. That's okay; just find another that suits the subject of your movie.

1 Double-click the title to open the Enter Text for Title screen.

2 Click Change the Text Font and Color.

The Select Title Font and Color screen opens. Most of the controls are like those in word processors.

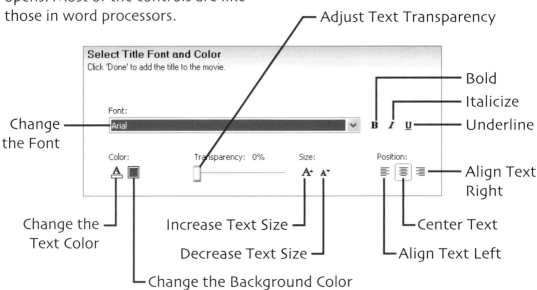

adjust fonts

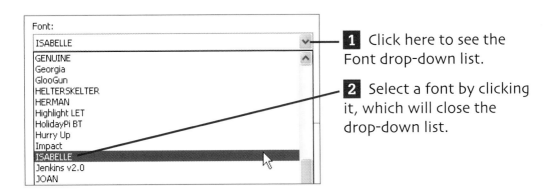

1 Click here to see the Font drop-down list.

2 Select a font by clicking it, which will close the drop-down list.

After you select the font, Movie Maker previews it in the Monitor. I'll show you ISABELLE looks after you change the background color.

3 Click the Change the Background Color icon.

adjust fonts (cont.)

4 Select the desired background color in the Color palette. Find a color that provides a good contrast with both the text and the background. Here I'm using blue.

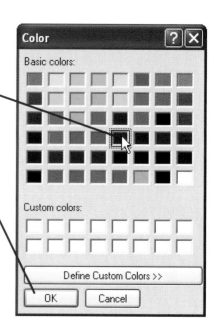

5 Click OK.

6 Movie Maker previews the title in the Monitor. After finalizing your selections, click Done (located below the font and background color buttons, at the left of the screen).

Here's the title after all adjustments. Gotta love the font, though the color may still be a touch neon. It's definitely readable, though, so I'm going to use this combination for all scene changes. Add titles for all of your scene changes. Movie Maker will continue to use the settings you apply here until you change them.

creating titles

add closing credits

Now add some closing credits.

1 In the Movie Tasks pane, click Make Titles or Credits.

2 Click Add Credits at the End of the Movie.

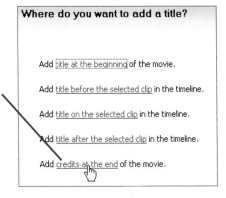

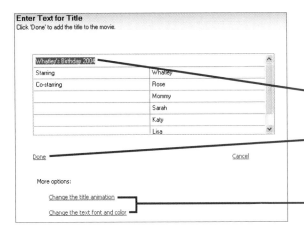

3 In the window that appears, type the desired text.

4 Click Done.

If desired, you can hunt for a different animation scheme or change the text font and colors by clicking here.

Here are my closing credits, a wonderfully suitable way to end this chapter.

extra bits

create an opening title p. 76

- Microsoft's free Creativity Fun Pack (http://www.microsoft.com/windowsxp/moviemaker/downloads/create.asp) provides three ways to enhance the visual appeal of your titles. First, it comes with 14 still images that you can use as static backgrounds for your text titles. Second, the pack includes two video backgrounds, one yellow, and one blue, which you can also use as backgrounds for your titles. Finally, the pack includes several videos designed for use at the beginning or end of your movie: for instance, the Countdown video counts down from five to zero and then flashes the word START.

change to title overlay p. 78

- You can apply transitions and effects to full-screen titles located on the Video track: for example, fading into the opening title of a movie or fading out of the closing credits. However, you can't apply either transitions or effects to titles on the Title Overlay track.

creating titles

8. using audio

Audio is an incredibly powerful medium. The right background music can set the proper mood for a movie or slide show and amuse and entertain in its own right, and narration can provide additional information and context to help the viewer appreciate the visual aspect of the presentation.

In this chapter, you'll add both background music and narration to your movie, and you'll learn how to integrate it smoothly with the audio you captured with your camcorder. Note that you can perform these activities only on the Timeline, not on the Storyboard.

Movie Maker has two audio tracks. The Audio track contains only audio captured with the video file.

The Audio/Music track contains all other audio, including narration and background music.

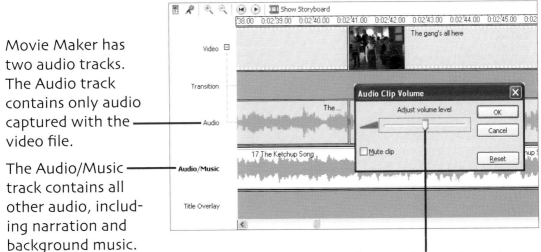

Here I'm about to lower the volume of the background music track so I can hear the conversation in the video more clearly.

add background music

Let's start by inserting some background music into the project. Find some music appropriate for your project and import it into a collection as described in Chapter 2.

1 In the Collections pane, click the collection that contains the audio file.

Movie Maker displays the collection in the Contents pane.

2 Click and drag the audio clip to the Audio/Music track.

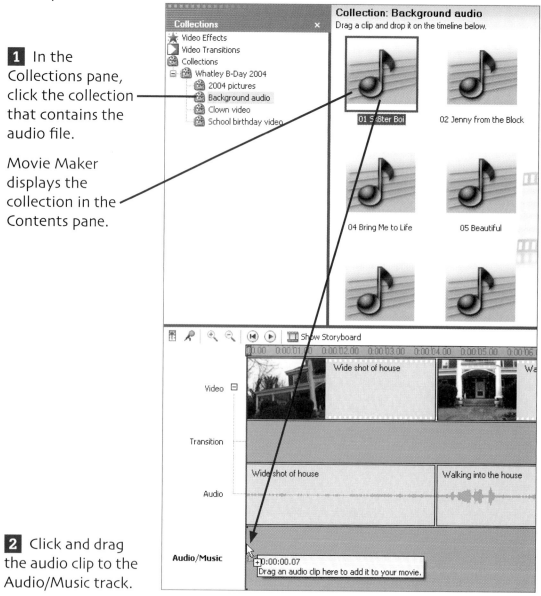

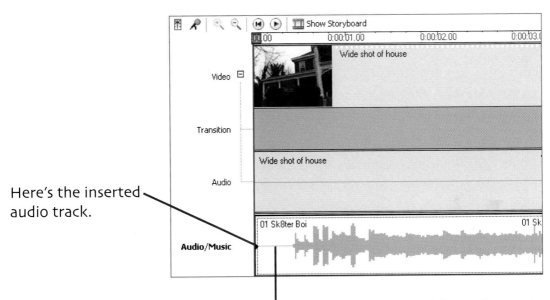

Here's the inserted audio track.

The flat line at the start of the audio track indicates that it's silent there. The silence is less than a second long, but to make the music start right away, the silence needs to be trimmed off.

trim audio clips

You trim audio clips like any other content: you simply grab an edge and drag it to the desired length.

1 Click the clip on the Timeline to select it.

2 Hover the mouse over the edge until the trim cursor appears.

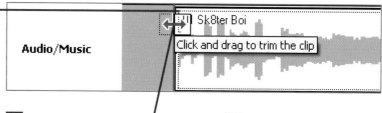

3 Click the mouse button and drag to the right (or left if you're trimming the end of the clip).

4 Release the mouse when the clip starts where you want it to.

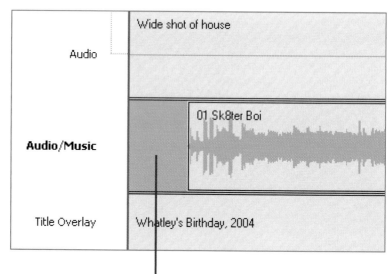

Movie Maker left a gap on the Audio/Music track when the clip was shortened. Unless the gap is removed, the audio won't start playing immediately.

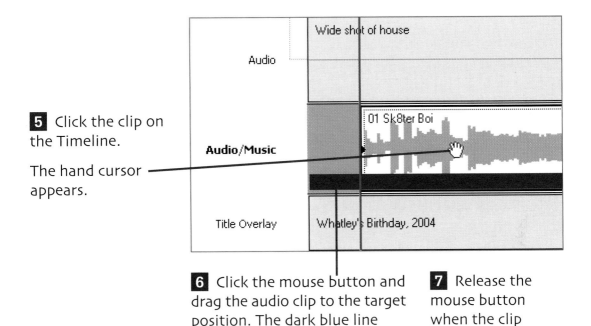

5 Click the clip on the Timeline.

The hand cursor appears.

6 Click the mouse button and drag the audio clip to the target position. The dark blue line below the audio clip shows the clip's new position as you drag.

7 Release the mouse button when the clip extends as far as you want it to.

The gap is filled, and the audio will start at the same time as the video.

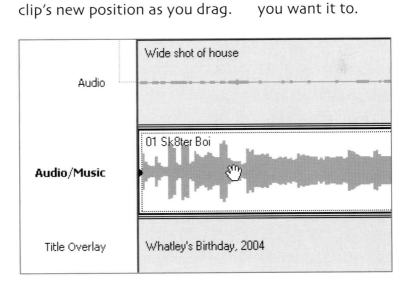

the big picture

Here's a big-picture view of how I want the background music to integrate with the audio from the camcorder.

Each track displays a waveform, which is a graphical representation of the audio file.

A small waveform indicates low volume.

A larger waveform indicates higher volume.

A mix of high and low volumes often indicates someone talking.

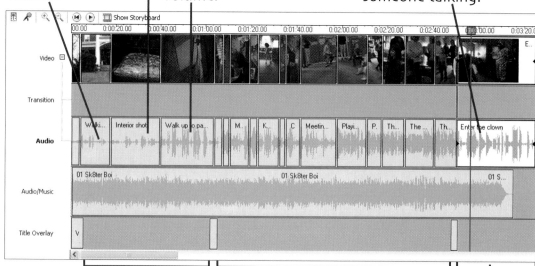

These are my outdoor and indoor establishing shots, which give the viewer the lay of the land. Here I want to turn off the audio on the Audio track (captured with the video) and solely use the background music track.

Here guests are arriving. Now I want primarily to hear the conversation, with the music track much lower in the background.

Now the clown starts performing, so I want to disable background audio completely so the audience can hear the show.

Your project will likely have scenes with similar characteristics: some where you want just the background music, some where you want just the audio that is part of your video, and some where you want a mix of both. Follow along to see how to make this happen.

mute the audio

Find a scene in your project that you want to mute (turn down the audio to 0%). I'm muting the Audio track for the opening scene of my movie.

1 Click the clips that you want to mute (hold down the Shift key to select multiple clips).

2 Right-click.

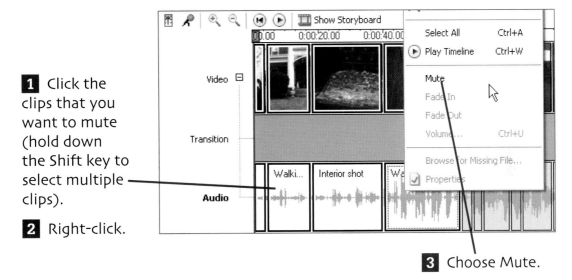

3 Choose Mute.

The flat line waveform indicates that Movie Maker muted the tracks.

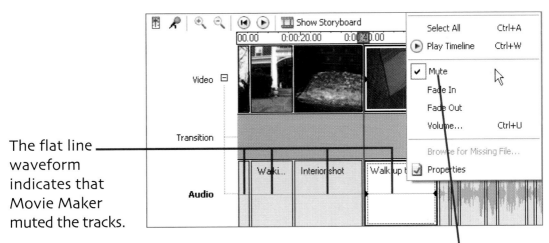

You can right-click and choose Mute again to unmute the track.

turn down music

Now find a scene where you want to turn down the background audio so you can hear the sound you recorded with your video. I want to turn down the background music in the second scene of my movie, so the conversations I recorded with the video can be heard. Since Movie Maker doesn't let you adjust the volume of just a portion of an audio clip, you first have to split the audio clip at the scene change. Then you can reduce the volume of the second part of the audio clip.

1 Click the audio clip to select it.

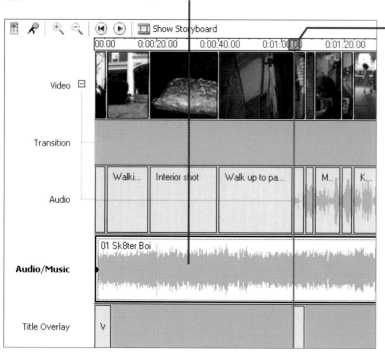

2 Move the Playback indicator to the start of the new scene.

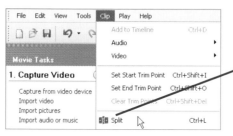

3 From Movie Maker's main menu, choose Clip > Split.

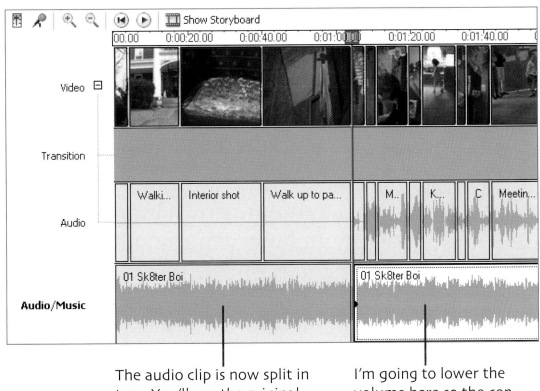

The audio clip is now split in
two. You'll use the original
volume on this segment.

I'm going to lower the
volume here so the con-
versation and other sound
in the video can be heard
more clearly.

adjust the volume

Now let's adjust the volume of the background music. Find a scene in your project where you've inserted background music, but also want your viewers to be able to hear the audio shot with the video.

1 Click the part of the split audio clip where you want to change the volume.

2 Right-click and choose Volume.

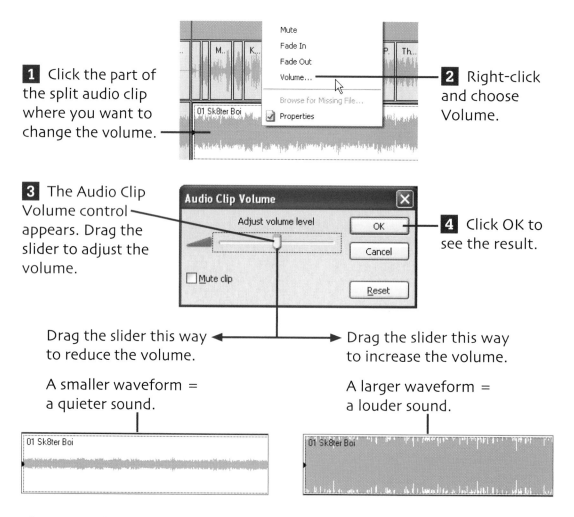

3 The Audio Clip Volume control appears. Drag the slider to adjust the volume.

4 Click OK to see the result.

Drag the slider this way to reduce the volume.

A smaller waveform = a quieter sound.

Drag the slider this way to increase the volume.

A larger waveform = a louder sound.

These waveforms are useful, but you'll really have to preview to hear the new levels. Keep adjusting the background music until you achieve the desired volume mix between the two tracks.

trim and fade audio

If you inserted background music into your movie, there may be a place where you want the music to stop playing, so that your audience hears only the audio you recorded with your video. In my movie, when the clown performs, I want the background music to stop, so the viewers can focus on the performance. Here's what to do.

Here's where the clown starts performing. This is where I want the background music to stop.

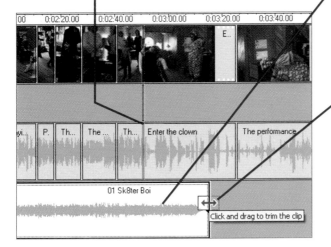

1 On the Audio/Music track, click the audio clip to select it.

2 Hover the mouse over the clip's edge until the trim cursor appears.

3 Click the mouse button and drag to the left to shorten the clip.

4 Release the mouse button when you reach the place where you want the background audio to end.

Now fade out the background audio so the ending isn't abrupt.

5 Click the background audio clip.

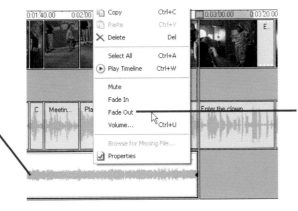

6 Right-click and choose Fade Out.

set up for narration

In Chapter 4, I built a slide show with digital pictures and music. Now I'm thinking it would be better to have my daughter narrate the slide show, putting the year's worth of pictures in her own words. I often add narrations to digital pictures and videos if the descriptions will enhance the viewing experience. Find a part of your own project that could use narration and give it a try.

To create your narration, you'll need a microphone. Here are two types of microphone you can use.

This is a universal serial bus (USB) microphone that connects to the computer's USB port.

This headset combines a microphone and headphones. The red plug always goes into the microphone connector, and the black plug goes into the speaker or headphone connector.

using audio

Connect the microphones to your computer. Here are the connections on my HP xw41000 computer.

Plug a USB microphone into one of the USB ports.

This is the headphone connector for a headset microphone; plug in the black connector here.

This is the microphone connector for a headset microphone; plug in the red plug here.

This is the FireWire port where you connect your camcorder for video capture.

create narration

1 On the Timeline, move the Playback indicator to the place where you want the narration to begin.

2 Click the Narrate Timeline button.

The Narrate Timeline window appears. Here's where you adjust the volume and start and stop recording.

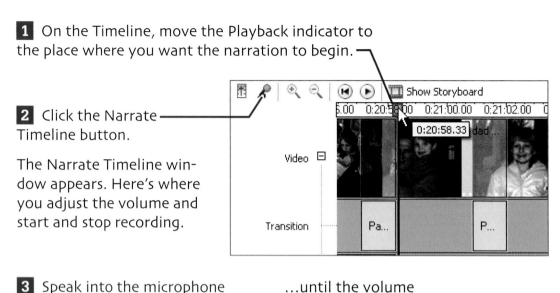

3 Speak into the microphone normally. Adjust the volume control...

...until the volume line stays consistently between 50 and 75%.

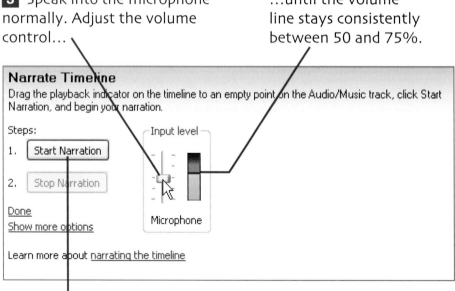

4 Click Start Narration to begin the narration. Movie Maker will start playing the video from the narration starting point so you can watch it in the Monitor as you record.

using audio

5 Start talking into the microphone.

Watch the volume meter so you stay within the 50 to 75% volume range.

6 Click Stop Narration when you're done. The Save Windows Media File dialog box appears.

Narrate Timeline

Drag the playback indicator on the timeline to an e
Narration, and begin your narration.

Steps: Input level

1.   Start Narration

2.   Stop Narration

Done
Show more options   Microphone

Learn more about narrating the timeline

create narration (cont.)

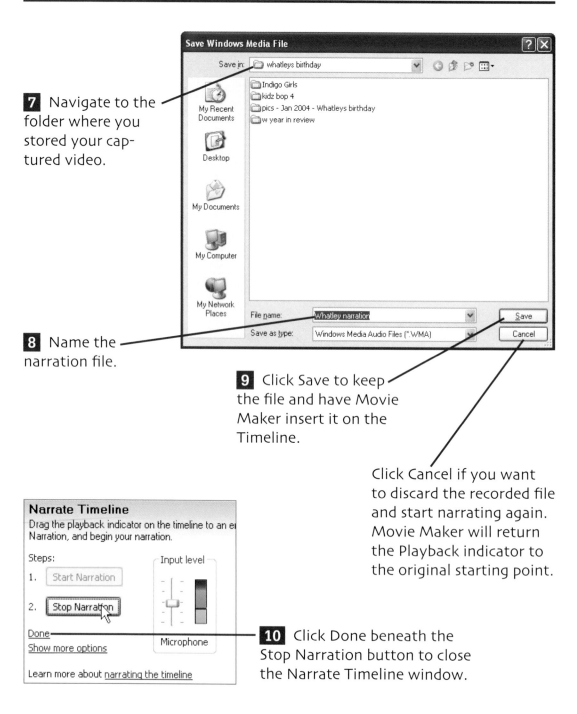

7 Navigate to the folder where you stored your captured video.

8 Name the narration file.

9 Click Save to keep the file and have Movie Maker insert it on the Timeline.

Click Cancel if you want to discard the recorded file and start narrating again. Movie Maker will return the Playback indicator to the original starting point.

10 Click Done beneath the Stop Narration button to close the Narrate Timeline window.

using audio

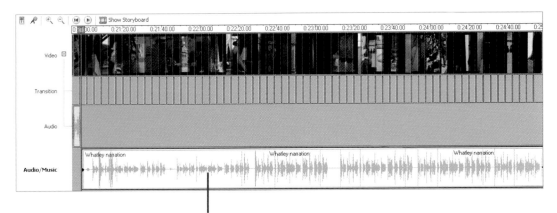

The completed narration
underneath the slide show.

extra bits

add background music p. 92

- I use Windows Media Player to copy audio tracks from a CD-ROM so I can include them in a movie. It's very simple to use, but if you want step-by-step guidance, see Microsoft Windows Movie Maker 2: Visual QuickStart Guide from Peachpit Press for details.

- You can also add sound effects to your videos on the Audio/Music track. Although Movie Maker doesn't come with any sound effects or background music, Microsoft offers two free sources of both. The Creativity Fun Pack (http://www.microsoft.com/windowsxp/moviemaker/downloads/create.asp) comes with 53 sound effects in five categories: animal, fun random, graduation, party and sports, and background music. Microsoft's Windows Movie Maker 2 Winter Fun Pack 2003 (http://www.microsoft.com/windowsxp/moviemaker/downloads/winterfun.asp), also free, includes 92 sound effects and 7 music tracks.

set up for narration p. 102

- There's a big difference between the microphone port and the line-in port available on some computers. The line-in port is used for the output from stereo systems and other independently powered devices and requires a significantly stronger signal than you get with the typical computer microphone. Line-in ports won't work with a microphone, so be sure you connect your microphone to the microphone port.

9. creating automovies

Music videos have been a powerful component of movies since the "Raindrops Keep Falling on My Head" bicycling scene in Butch Cassidy and the Sundance Kid (boy am I dating myself). Movie Maker makes it simple to build such a scene with the AutoMovie feature.

AutoMovie takes your video, trims away all but the most interesting short clips, and synchronizes the clips with a song that you select. It's almost like having an MTV music video producer inside your computer. It's fast, it's fun, and the results can be surprisingly compelling.

Here's the AutoMovie I'll build in this chapter. Note the short video clips as trimmed by Movie Maker and the inserted transitions and titles on their respective tracks.

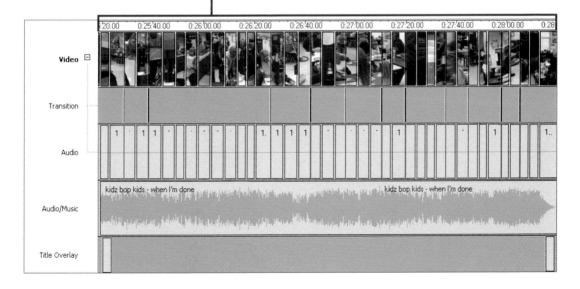

build an automovie

Yikes! Whatley looked over the movie while creating the narration in the last chapter and asked, "Where's the footage from the party at school?" Ruh-roh, daddy forgot, and I'm running out of editing time. Rather than manually edit that party, I'll create an AutoMovie and add it to the project. Grab a stretch of your own video footage and a favorite tune and join in.

Note that Movie Maker places any AutoMovies you create at the end of the project.

1 In the Contents pane, choose the video clips you want to include in the AutoMovie. Press the Shift key to choose multiple consecutive clips, and the Ctrl key to choose multiple noncontiguous clips.

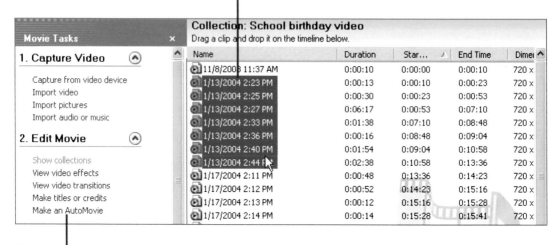

2 In the Movie Tasks pane, click Make an AutoMovie.

3 In the Select an AutoMovie Editing Style window that opens, click the desired editing style. The editing style controls the nature of the effects and transitions Movie Maker applies and the pace of the video. I've always liked the Music Video style, so try that one.

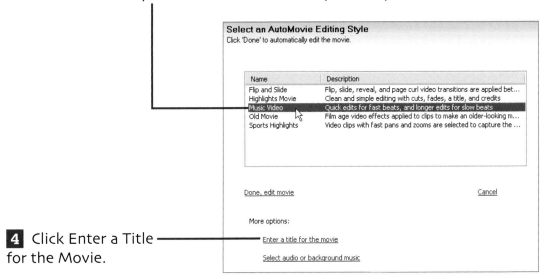

4 Click Enter a Title for the Movie.

5 In the Enter Text for Title window that opens, type the title text.

Note that each style has specific font and color options that you can't modify.

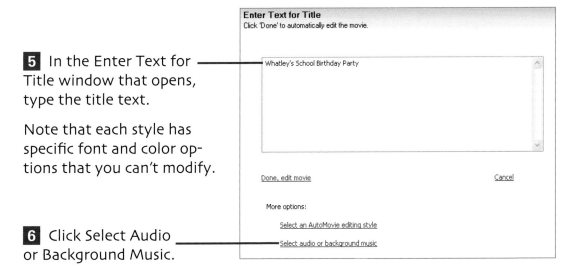

6 Click Select Audio or Background Music.

build an automovie (cont.)

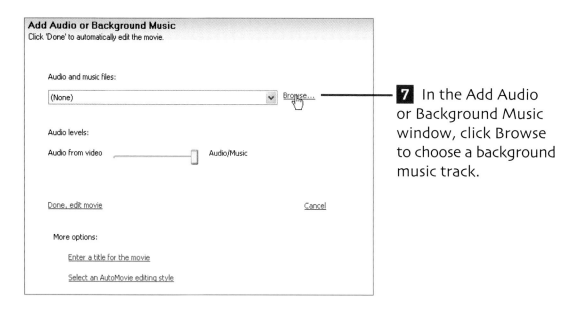

7 In the Add Audio or Background Music window, click Browse to choose a background music track.

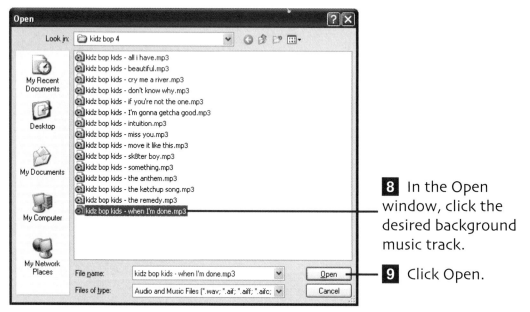

8 In the Open window, click the desired background music track.

9 Click Open.

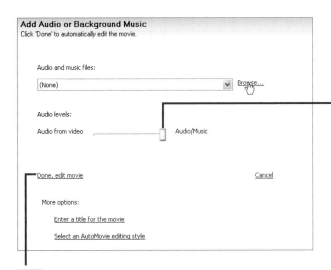

10 In the Add Audio or Background Music window, drag the Audio Levels slider all the way to the right, to 100% Audio/Music.

AutoMovie doesn't work well if you want to hear what people are saying, because it tends to randomly cut people off in mid-sentence. I never use this feature when I want to hear the audio shot with the video.

11 Click Done, Edit Movie. Movie Maker builds the AutoMovie and inserts it at the end of the Timeline.

Here's the finished AutoMovie. All video segments are very short.

Movie Maker muted the audio on the Audio track.

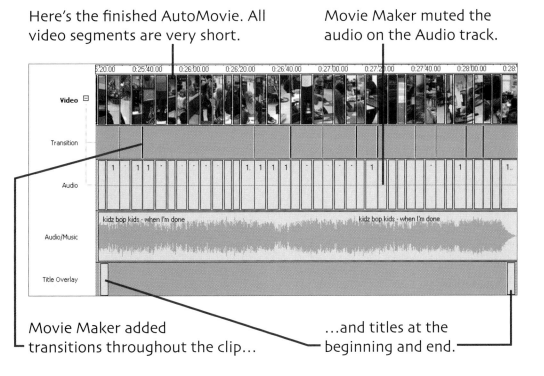

Movie Maker added transitions throughout the clip...

...and titles at the beginning and end.

extra bits

build an automovie p. 110

- Play yor AutoMovie right away after you create it, and if you don't like it, simply click Undo to make it go away and then start over. Otherwise, you'll have to delete all the parts manually, which can take a while.

- After Movie Maker produces the AutoMovie, you can edit any component as desired.

- If your footage contains any clips or portions of clips that you absolutely don't want included in the AutoMovie, delete them in the Contents pane before producing the AutoMovie. See Chapter 3 for details.

10. that's a wrap

You've finished your project, and now it's time to show it off to the world. The challenge, of course, is that the world is a big place, so you may need to deliver the video in different formats over different media.

Fortunately, Movie Maker offers a range of output formats. Figure out which ones work for you and then follow along.

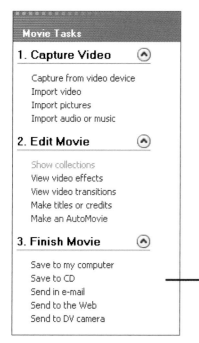

No matter how you intend to send your movie to your target audience, it all starts here in the Movie Tasks pane.

save on computer

I keep a copy of most movies I produce on my editing station, if only to amuse my daughters when they're spending time in my office. If you plan on playing the finished movie on the computer that produced it, this is the best option.

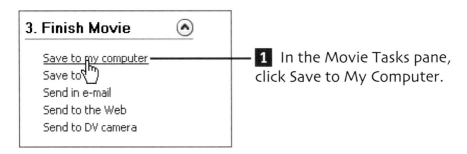

1 In the Movie Tasks pane, click Save to My Computer.

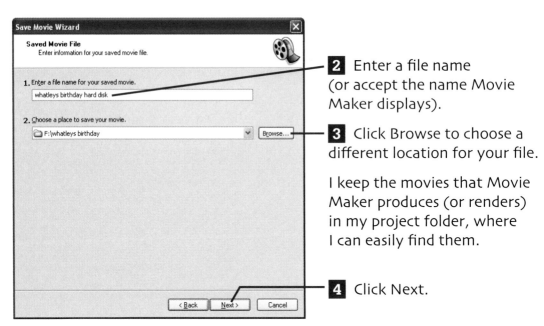

2 Enter a file name (or accept the name Movie Maker displays).

3 Click Browse to choose a different location for your file.

I keep the movies that Movie Maker produces (or renders) in my project folder, where I can easily find them.

4 Click Next.

that's a wrap

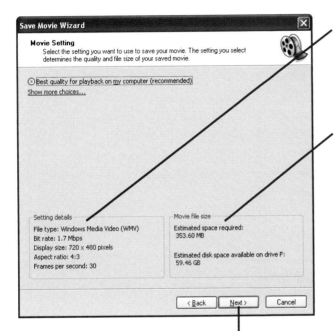

The Setting Details area shows the default output parameters Movie Maker uses to produce videos for playback on your computer.

The Movie File Size area reports the size of the rendered file and remaining hard disk space. If disk space is insufficient, Movie Maker will tell you and won't let you continue.

5 Click Next to start encoding— the process during which Movie Maker produces the digital file.

save on computer (cont.)

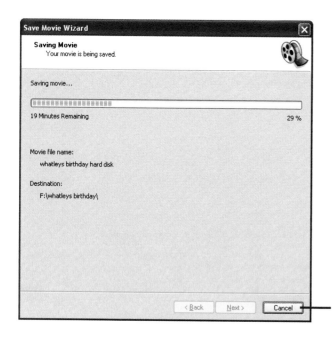

My project is about 28 minutes long and took about 33 minutes to produce on a 3.2 GHz Pentium 4 HP xw4100 workstation. Your mileage will definitely vary by processor speed, with slower machines taking much longer.

Click Cancel if you want to stop the encoding.

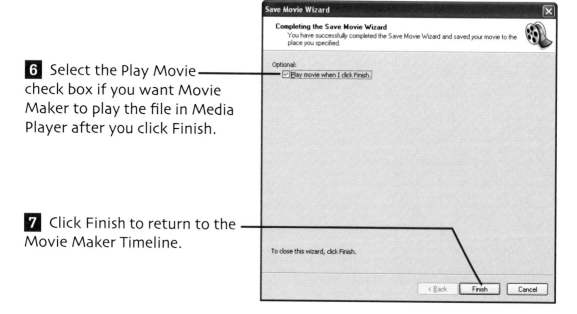

6 Select the Play Movie check box if you want Movie Maker to play the file in Media Player after you click Finish.

7 Click Finish to return to the Movie Maker Timeline.

that's a wrap

save on cd

You may also want to burn your movie file to a CD to archive it or to send it to a friend or relative.

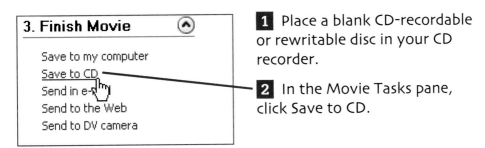

1 Place a blank CD-recordable or rewritable disc in your CD recorder.

2 In the Movie Tasks pane, click Save to CD.

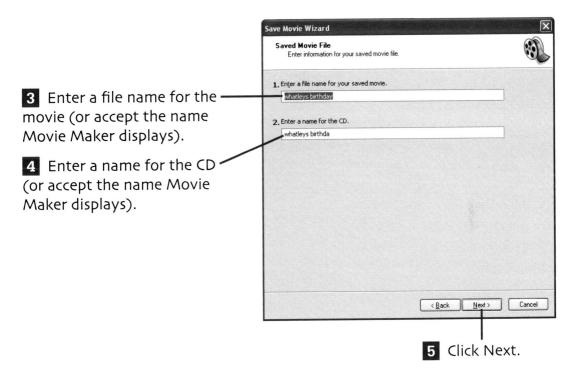

3 Enter a file name for the movie (or accept the name Movie Maker displays).

4 Enter a name for the CD (or accept the name Movie Maker displays).

5 Click Next.

save on cd (cont.)

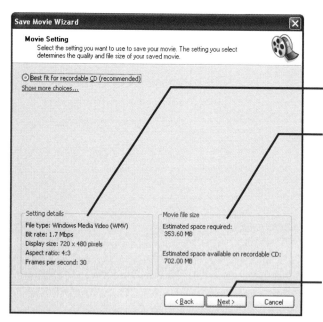

The Setting Details area shows the default output parameters Movie Maker uses to produce videos for burning to CD-ROM.

The Movie File Size area tells you the size of the file and the capacity of the CD-recordable disc. If the space is insufficient for your project, Movie Maker will tell you and won't let you continue.

6 Click Next to continue.

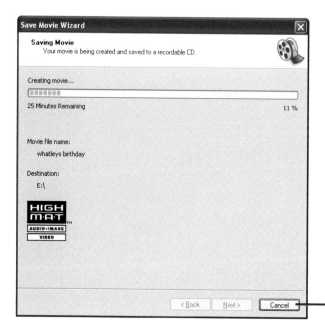

Movie Maker is encoding the file. When encoding is done, Movie Maker will burn the file to the CD-R. The CD-R should play on virtually all current Windows and Macintosh computers and on any HighMAT-compatible consumer electronics device.

Click Cancel if you want to stop the process.

that's a wrap

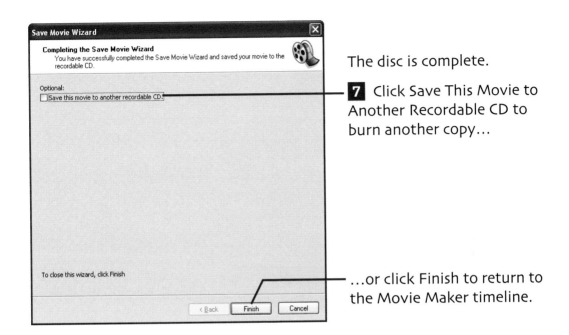

The disc is complete.

7 Click Save This Movie to Another Recordable CD to burn another copy...

...or click Finish to return to the Movie Maker timeline.

send in e-mail

My project is fairly long; if yours is similarly long, sending via e-mail won't be an option (as you'll see in a moment). However, for shorter projects, say around 3 minutes or less, e-mail is a great way to send movies to friends and family.

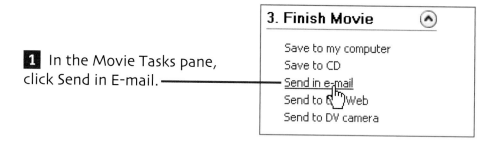

1 In the Movie Tasks pane, click Send in E-mail.

3. Finish Movie

Save to my computer
Save to CD
Send in e-mail
Send to the Web
Send to DV camera

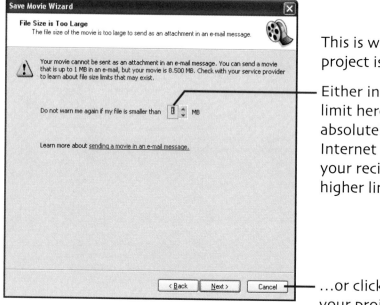

This is what you'll see if your project is too long.

Either increase the file size limit here (but only if you are absolutely certain that your Internet service provider and your recipient's accept the higher limit)...

...or click Cancel and shorten your project to around 3 minutes or less.

that's a wrap

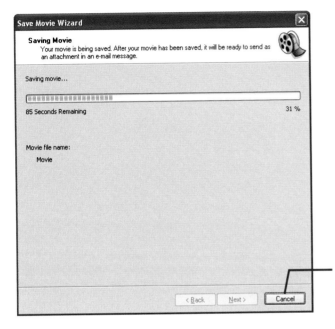

If your project is short enough to send via e-mail, Movie Maker will immediately start encoding.

Click Cancel if you want to stop the process.

Rendering is complete.

Click here if you want to play the movie.

Click here if you want to save the movie to your hard disk.

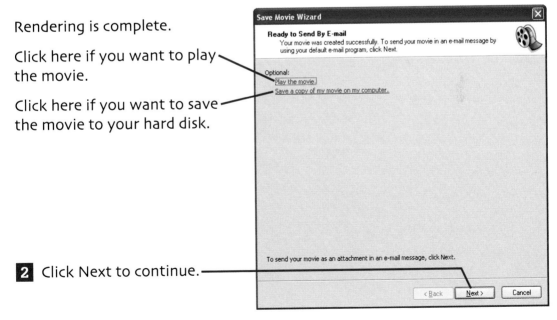

2 Click Next to continue.

send in e-mail (cont.)

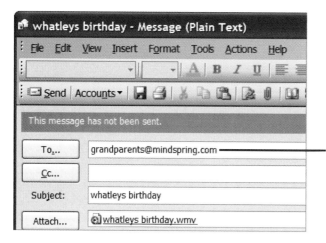

Movie Maker opens your e-mail program, opens a new message, and inserts the rendered file as an attachment.

3 Enter an e-mail recipient and message as desired and send the e-mail as you normally would.

that's a wrap

upload to the web

Use this option to send video files to www.neptune.com or other Web hosting services supported by Movie Maker (as I write, Neptune is the only supported service). Once you've uploaded your project (and joined Neptune), you can invite others to view your video from the pages that Neptune supplies. Neptune offers a free three-day trial account and a one-year membership for $59. You'll need an Internet connection and a trial membership with Neptune to complete the process described here. (To set up a trial account, go to www.neptune.com.)

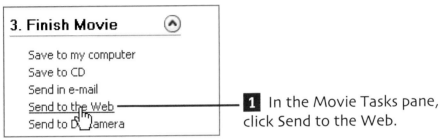

1 In the Movie Tasks pane, click Send to the Web.

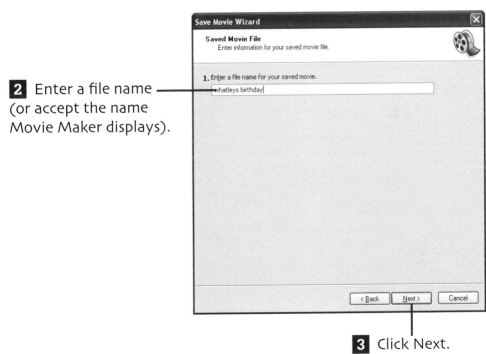

2 Enter a file name (or accept the name Movie Maker displays).

3 Click Next.

upload to the web (cont.)

4 Select the connection speed used by the person who will watch the video over the Internet. If you're not sure, select Dial Up Modem.

The files uploaded to the Neptune Web site are much smaller than those produced for viewing from your hard disk or CD-ROM (160x120 as opposed to 720x480), which means they won't look quite as good. This reduction in display size is necessary to ensure that the video plays smoothly over the connection speed used by your viewers.

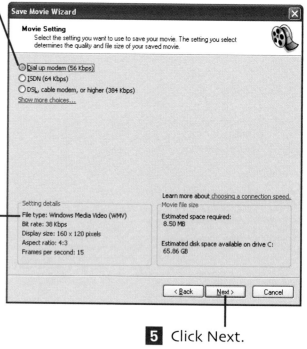

5 Click Next.

Movie Maker starts encoding your file.

Click Cancel if you want to stop encoding. After it finishes encoding, Movie Maker automatically advances to the next screen in the wizard.

that's a wrap

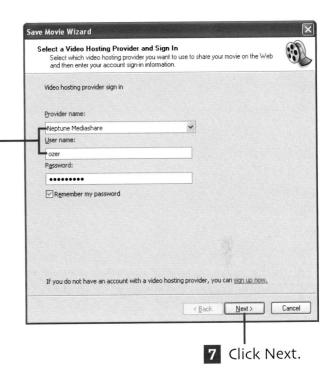

6 Select a provider and enter a user name and password.

If desired, click the Remember My Password check box to avoid having to log in during future sessions.

7 Click Next.

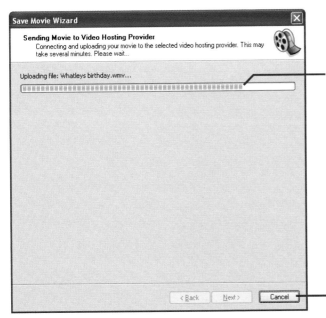

Movie Maker starts uploading the file to Neptune.

Click Cancel if you want to stop uploading. After it finishes uploading, Movie Maker automatically advances to the next screen in the wizard.

that's a wrap

upload to the web (cont.)

8 Click the Watch My Movie on the Web After I Click Finish check box to view your file on the Web after you click Finish.

9 Click Finish.

Movie Maker opens your browser to your Neptune home page.

that's a wrap

save on tape

I write all my Movie Maker projects back to tape, usually for archival purposes, but sometimes to copy (or dub) the movie to VHS tape for viewers who don't have computers. This is probably a good idea for you as well. Start by going back to Set Up for DV Capture in Chapter 2 and getting your DV camera connected and ready. Then proceed as decsribed here.

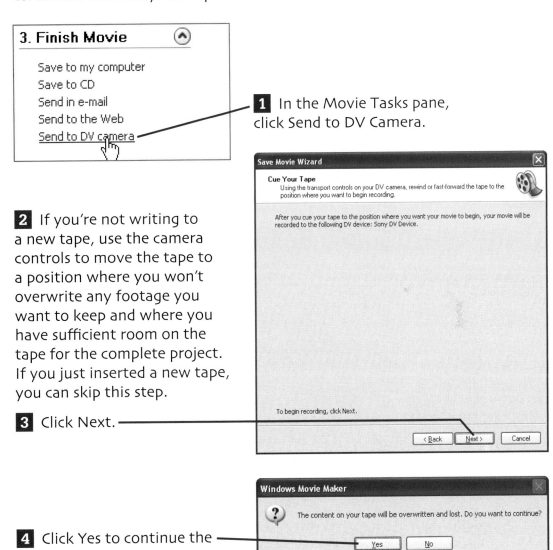

1 In the Movie Tasks pane, click Send to DV Camera.

2 If you're not writing to a new tape, use the camera controls to move the tape to a position where you won't overwrite any footage you want to keep and where you have sufficient room on the tape for the complete project. If you just inserted a new tape, you can skip this step.

3 Click Next.

4 Click Yes to continue the process.

save on tape (cont.)

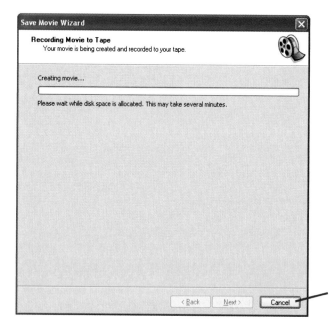

Movie Maker starts rendering your project and then writing the video back to tape.

Click Cancel if you want to cancel the process.

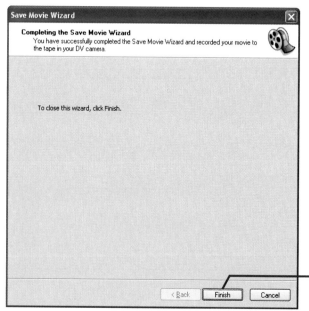

5 Click Finish to return to the Movie Maker Timeline.

that's a wrap

save to create dvd

After producing my movies in Movie Maker, I sometimes create DVDs of the movies, usually with Sonic Solutions MyDVD, an inexpensive yet highly functional program. When producing a DVD, I want to start with the best possible file, so I render back to DV video, the highest-quality format Movie Maker can output. If you're producing a file to include on a DVD, render the file as described here.

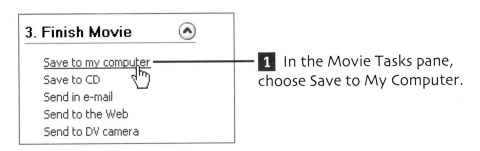

1 In the Movie Tasks pane, choose Save to My Computer.

2 Enter a file name (or accept the name Movie Maker displays).

3 Click Browse to choose a different location for your file.

I keep rendered files in my project folder where I can easily find them.

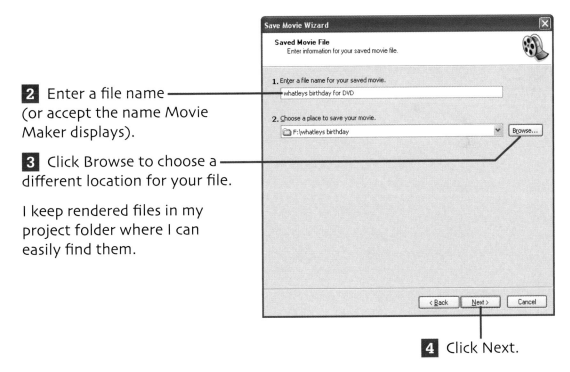

4 Click Next.

save to create dvd (cont.)

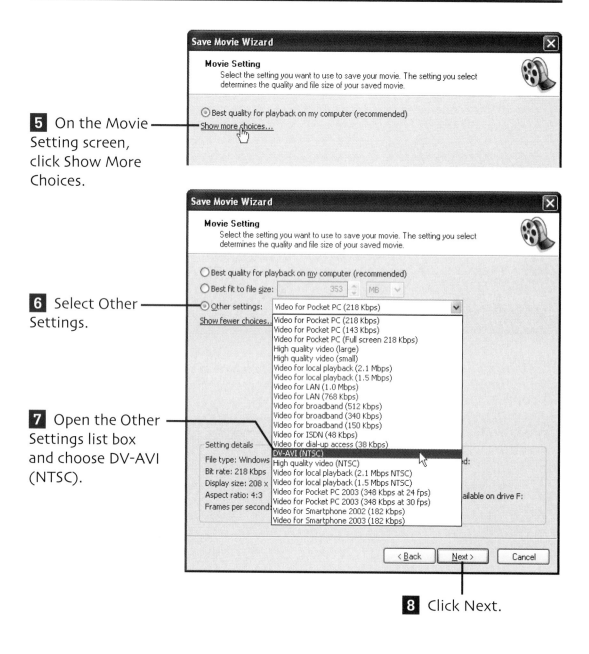

5 On the Movie Setting screen, click Show More Choices.

6 Select Other Settings.

7 Open the Other Settings list box and choose DV-AVI (NTSC).

8 Click Next.

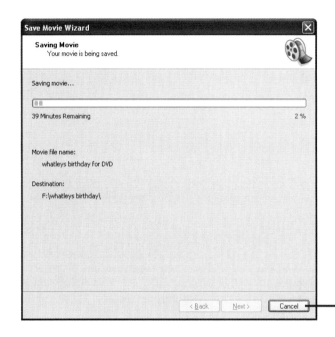

Movie Maker starts encoding.

Click Cancel if you want to stop the encoding.

All done.

9 Select the Play Movie check box if you want Movie Maker to play the file in Media Player after you click Finish.

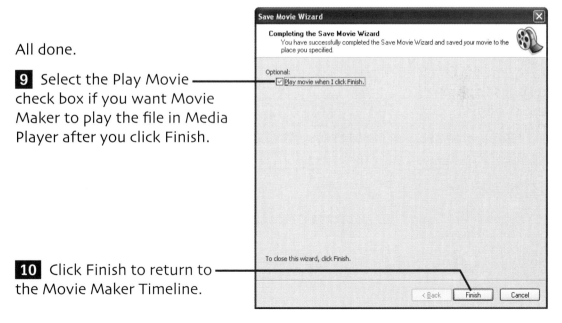

10 Click Finish to return to the Movie Maker Timeline.

extra bits

save on cd p. 119

- Most DVD recorders can also write to CD-recordable media. Movie Maker can write to a DVD recorder with CD-recordable media loaded, but it can't write to a DVD recorder with DVD-recordable media loaded.

- Movie Maker can store about one hour of video on a CD using the techniques described in this chapter.

- HighMAT is a Microsoft-sponsored format designed to allow one CD-recordable disc to play on consumer electronics devices and computers. At the time of this writing, only a few consumer electronics devices support this format, and I don't own one. Thus, I use Movie Maker's Save to CD function solely to produce discs for playback on computers.

send in e-mail p. 122

- I do most of my e-mailing from my Dell laptop rather than my encoding station, so I use the Save a Copy of My Movie on My Computer option to save an e-mail-sized file, which I transfer to the Dell over my network and then e-mail from there.

save on tape p. 129

- If you're interested in learning more about how to dub your movies from DV to VHS tape, check out Microsoft Windows Movie Maker 2: Visual QuickStart Guide, also published by Peachpit Press, where this process is described in detail.

that's a wrap

index

index

commands
    Clip menu, Split, 98
    Edit menu, Select All, 48
    File menu
        Import into Collections, 17
        Save Movie File, 42
        Save Project As, 42
    Tools menu, Options, 6
compression, codecs, 6
contents, 2, 9. See also project
    assets
    collections. See collections
    DV (Digital Video) capture,
       10–14
    importing
        audio, 19–20
        pictures, 17–18
        video, 21–22
    saving, 42, 48
    setting options, 6–7
Contents pane, 2–3
    audio, 91
        background music, 92–93
        clips, xviii
            trimming, 94–95, 101
        fading, 101
        formats, 23
        importing, 19–20
        muting, 97
        narration
            creating, 104–107
            set up, 102–103
        transition, fade in/out, 56,
            61
        turning down volume,
            98–99
        volume adjustment, 100
        waveforms, 96
    pictures, xviii. See also images
        capture, 10–14
        formats, 23
        importing, 17–18
        inserting, 43
        saving movies, 129–130
    transitions, 49, 60, xi
        audio fade in/out, 56, 61
        changing, 54
        dissolve insertion, 51–52

duration, 55
    previewing, 50, 53
    repeat, 58–59
    titles, 90
    video fade to black, 57, 61
videos, xviii
    clips
        brightening special
            effect, 66
        deleting, 26
        DV (Digital Video)
            capture, 10–14
        trimming, 40
    formats, 23
    importing, 21–22
    size, 7
    transition fade to black,
       57, 61
Create Clips check box, 13

D

dates, naming conventions, 23
Decrease Text Size control (Select
    Title Font and Color screen),
    86
dialog boxes
    Add or Remove Video Effects,
       69
    Import File, 17
    Options, 7
    Save Windows Media File, 105
digital cameras
    adding pictures to movie, xii
    project requirements, xvi
Digital Video (DV)
    capture, 10–14
    saving movies, 129–130
disk space, project requirements,
    xvi
dissolve transitions, 51–52
downloads
    Move Maker, 8
    special effects Web site, 73
    transitions Web site, 61
duration settings, 7–8
    adjusting, 47

titles, 83
transitions, 55
DV (Digital Video)
    capture, 10–14
    saving movies, 129–130
DV-AVI format, 11
DVDs, saving movies, 131–133

E

e-mail
    sending movies, 122–124
    video size, 7
Ease In effect, 71–72
Edit menu commands, Select All,
    48
effects, 63
    brightening video clips, 66
    download Web site, 73
    fade video in/out, 65, 73
    motion effects, 71–74
    playback speed, 70, 74
    previewing, 64, 67–68
    removing, 69
Enter Text for Title screen, 82
extrabits, xv

F

fading
    audio, 101
        transition, 56
    video
        special effects in/out, 65, 73
        transition, 57, 61
File menu commands
    Import into Collections, 17
    Save Movie File, 42
    Save Project As, 42
files, storage, 6
FireWire
    cable project requirements, xvii
    card project requirements, xvi
    ports, 10
Font control (Select Title Font and
    Color screen), 86

index

index   **139**

Ready to Learn More?